PERFECTLY LEGAL
TAX LOOPHOLES

PERFECTLY LEGAL Tax £OOPHOLES

STEPHEN COURTNEY

PIATKUS

Disclaimer
The views contained herein are put forward for further consideration only, and are not to be acted upon without independent consideration and professional advice regarding any particular matter and the law and practice prevailing aᵗ the time. Neither the publishers nor the author can accept any responsibility for any loss occasioned to any person, no matter howsoever caused or arising as a result of or in consequence of action taken or refrained from being taken in reliance of the contents hereof.

First published in 1992 by
Judy Piatkus (Publishers) Ltd of
5 Windmill Street, London W1P 1HF

**The moral right of the author
has been asserted**

*A catalogue record for this book is available
from the British Library*

ISBN 0-7499-1145-X
ISBN 0-7499-1150-6 (pbk)

Edited by Carol Franklin
Designed by Paul Saunders

Set in Linotron Plantin Light by
Computerset Ltd, Harmondsworth
Printed and bound in Great Britain by
Biddles Ltd, Guildford & King's Lynn

CONTENTS

PREFACE

I have written this book as a result of the numerous letters and comments I received after the publication of my first book, *Taxman Tactics* (Sidgwick & Jackson, 1990). *Taxman Tactics* was not devoted to tax saving; it merely set out to explain how the tax system works and how, if you understand the system, you can use it to your advantage. It explained how you could stay out of trouble with the taxman and how, if you inadvertently tiptoed into difficulties, you could extricate yourself with a minimum of fuss, bother and cost. To that extent it was unusual.

This book is not about tactics – it is about saving tax. However, I hope that it is equally unusual. I have deliberately set out to show that the highly complex, and sometimes impenetrable, tax legislation can be turned on its head or otherwise used in ways that the Inland Revenue did not intend when they introduced the rules.

I have not eschewed the simple and possibly familiar areas of saving tax; a tax saving is no less valuable and satisfying just because it is simple to obtain. However, most of the matters I discuss will not be so well known and I hope that even the hardened tax professional will find something of value within its pages.

I have tried to avoid a mere summary of the tax rules, which can be found in numerous other annual tax guides. But some background explanations are needed, for example in Chapter 5 on trusts, because without an understanding of what a trust is and how it works (and the different variety of trusts), you may find it difficult to follow some of the more significant loopholes.

I have also tried to avoid the constant temptation to be diverted from the exposure of a tax loophole into a discussion of tax pitfalls. That subject deserves another book all to itself. Where there is danger I have tried to alert you to how it can be avoided, but I have deliberately concentrated on the positive aspects of using loopholes in the legislation to save tax, rather than the more negative approach of simply pointing out what you cannot do.

You will be able to use many of these ideas yourself, but others will need professional advice if they are to be fully effective. I do not regard this as a shortcoming, because it is obviously unrealistic to expect a book of this size and nature to deal with every conceivable technical aspect of each idea. Instead, I have tried to highlight opportunities so that they can be pursued further in the light of the special circumstances of each individual case. The key to tax saving is to be aware of the opportunities and to take them when they arise – or better still to rearrange your circumstances to create an opportunity.

Tax loopholes are essentially mistakes in the legislation which were not appreciated even by the highly trained tax experts in the Inland Revenue. You cannot, therefore, expect it to be too easy to drive the occasional coach and horses through such complex legislation. Also, please bear in mind that some of these loopholes might ultimately be blocked – and other new ones appear.

The General Election and the Budget

This book went to press after the results of the General Election were known, and contains the rates of tax and allowances announced in the Conservative budget of 10 March 1992. However, I have ignored the changes whereby the first £2000 of taxable income is charged at 20% on the grounds that in the context of this book it should not make any difference.

A word is appropriate for those who are sensitive to sexist modes of expression. To keep things simple I have usually assumed that it is a husband who has the business, or is the person with the high income or with the substantial wealth. There is only limited statistical justification for this assumption, but to express every idea and example using a neutral gender would impair comprehension. If you prefer to substitute the feminine gender wherever the masculine gender appears, the sense should not be affected, nor should it lead to error or misunderstanding of the techniques discussed.

I am indebted to all my clients and colleagues, without whom I would never have had the incentive to dig deep into the tax legislation to find ways round their many and varied tax problems. Although I should like it to be otherwise, I cannot claim that all the ideas are of my own creation; in any specialist profession it is necessary to be aware of and to learn from the keen and more able minds of colleagues and friends – not to steal their ideas, but to be stimulated by their imagination and evolve solutions of one's own.

Finally, special thanks are due to my secretary Deirdre for her skill and patience in converting endless tapes into the appropriate electronic impulses without losing her sense of humour, and to the three little Courtneys who have forgone much of the attention they deserved but who have learnt the hard way that Daddy has to do homework as well.

Stephen Courtney
London
March 1992

=1=

TAX AND TAX AVOIDANCE

Everybody wants to save tax. Unfortunately the tax system is rather complicated and this makes saving tax rather difficult. After all, the government wants everybody to pay tax and does its level best to make sure they do. They make the rules and they enforce the rules, so you might think that the whole idea of trying to save tax is hopeless. This is not so, but it is complicated.

There are two main reasons why tax is so complicated. The most obvious reason is that because everybody is so keen to save tax, the rules keep being changed to block up all the loopholes as soon as they are found. The other reason, which is much more important for us, is that the government really wants to have a fair tax system, so they provide lots of allowances and reliefs to avoid hardship. An unfair tax system creates unrest and in the end the government will be voted out – or worse there would be an outbreak of civil disobedience to force a change. If you doubt the truth of these statements you only have to look at what happened with the poll tax in 1990 to see how public opinion can have an overwhelming effect on the imposition of a tax.

While nobody likes paying tax, everybody appreciates that taxes need to be paid, and as long as the system is broadly fair people will abide by it and pay their taxes regularly. This has been the position in Britain for a long time, which is why our system is so highly regarded and why our Inland Revenue is thought of as being one of the best in the world. Nobody would ever dream of trying to bribe one of Her Majesty's Inspectors of Taxes, still less expect that they could succeed. The esteem in which Inland Revenue officials are held means that the tax system has a much better chance of working – and it does.

However, a necessary consequence of a system which tries to accommodate everybody's widely differing circumstances fairly is the provision of numerous reliefs and allowances. Wherever there is a relief from tax, there is an opportunity to use it for your own benefit. If you can arrange your circumstances so that you fall within the relief, it must be given to you – even if you are not the type of person that the government originally intended to benefit from the relief.

Unfortunately, the position becomes further distorted because tax is also used as a means of economic and social control. The tax charge on cigarettes is (at least partly) designed to discourage smoking; a reduced tax charge on unleaded petrol encourages the use of unleaded petrol; and a tax relief such as the business expansion scheme encourages investment in new businesses. These are just three examples, but there are countless others – all designed to create something good or discourage something bad in our society. But with complications comes opportunity, and the purpose of this book is to explain the possibilities which exist for tax saving – *simply by using the rules to your advantage*.

The most important point is to *use* the rules – not break them. That is what this book is all about. Sometimes I will simply draw attention to reliefs which are genuinely intended by the tax system, and sometimes I will deal with circumstances which were certainly *not* intended when the tax rules were drafted. These unintended opportunities are often called loopholes, but that gives an impression that you are pulling a fast one over the Inland Revenue. That impression is false and dangerous. Playing games with the Inland Revenue is not generally recommended. Inspectors of Taxes are human too and if you try and be too clever they will probably not take too kindly – and they will almost certainly have the power and skill to defeat you.

The fact that some loopholes are actually intended should not be overlooked. It has been said that it is the loopholes which allow the tax system to breathe. But whatever you call them, or however you view the position, the result ought to be the same. Use the rules and stay within them and you will end up with more of your money in your pocket and less in the pocket of the Inland Revenue. After all, as long ago as 1929 Lord Clyde, in a tax case, set down the following principle:

> No man in this country is under the smallest obligation moral or other, to arrange his legal relations to his business or to his property so as to enable the Inland Revenue to put the largest shovel into his stores. The Inland Revenue is not slow – and quite rightly – to take every advantage which is open to it under the taxing statutes for the purpose of depleting the taxpayer's pocket. And the taxpayer is in like manner entitled to be as astute to prevent as far as he honestly can, the depletion of his means by the Inland Revenue.

Finally, I should say a word about professional advice and professional fees. Where matters are complex and the sums involved are large it is unreasonable to expect any book to provide a complete answer. Professional advice will probably be required, but that should not put anybody off. It is much better to pay professional fees than to pay the tax. However, you do have to be sure that the fees will be less than the tax saving – or worse, that you do not end up paying both the fees *and* the tax. These are matters which should be discussed with your professional adviser before issuing any instructions (or incurring any fee), and no reputable professional adviser will mind these points being made.

It should also be borne in mind that you are not much further forward if your professional adviser only says 'No, you cannot save the tax'. You can get that advice free from the Inland Revenue. You need to find a professional adviser who says 'Yes, you can save the tax'. He might start by saying that you cannot do what you had in mind, but you can do something else instead. Or he may say that you can only save part of the tax. It would be rare that your particular tax problem is utterly incapable of solution. Sometimes the possible solutions may be unacceptable for personal or financial reasons, but there will nearly always be something you can do.

Knowing the Rules

The payment of tax is not some kind of divine penance or even a natural state of affairs. It is the law. There is no morality involved – it is just the law. Like all laws it needs to be obeyed and penalties are imposed if you break it. However, it is a funny kind of law. Most laws are designed to make society run more smoothly by imposing a code of conduct to prevent us from harming our neighbours. Tax is designed simply to deprive us of some of our money and consequently it is a very sensitive matter. The fear is that if the government can deprive people of their property without very good reason, they can do other things as well such as deprive us of our liberty or even our lives, so the rules are taken very seriously indeed by those who make them to protect our freedom.

What this means is that paying tax is never arbitrary. It is closely regulated and the Inland Revenue is not entitled to a penny more than the law provides. To their credit Inspectors of Taxes do not try to obtain more – although they sometimes ask for more by mistake. Knowing the rules enables you to spot any mistakes and avoid paying tax when it is not properly due.

Sometimes you will hear it said that people 'ought' to pay tax. What this usually means is that other people ought to pay tax – but not me, please. That cannot be a basis for any rule of law; the same rules must apply to everybody. For the same reason the rules must be certain – although it can be extremely difficult to be certain what they mean most of the time.

Another misunderstanding is that everybody should pay their fair share of tax, because if one person does not pay it, everybody else has to pay more. Again, this is quite wrong. Leaving

4

aside the impossible judgement about what is a 'fair share' and what is not, it presupposes that all taxes are needed to meet expenditure. Of course, taxes are needed to meet expenditure, but that is only one of the reasons why they are raised. Tax is an important element in economic policy. I have already mentioned various types of activity which can be encouraged or discouraged by imposing taxes or the giving of tax reliefs. These have nothing to do with whether or not the income is actually needed.

What is equally important to understand is that tax is a way of taking money out of circulation. Low taxes mean that more money is in the hands of consumers who will spend it and that can cause inflation. If the government is worried about inflation being created by consumer spending, it can simply increase taxes and take our money away. Again, this has nothing to do with whether the government actually *wants* the money.

One final – and I think important – point is that high taxes can in fact *reduce* the amount of tax collected by the government. When rates are high, people go to great lengths to avoid paying them, but when rates go down there is less incentive to do so and many more people simply pay up. A lot of people paying a smaller amount of tax will result in more tax being received!

High rates of tax are therefore not necessarily imposed to raise revenue, but can be levied to promote a social or political purpose entirely unconnected to the amount of money which may be collected. For these and other reasons the idea that one person's tax saving is another person's tax bill is entirely wrong.

What about the Morals of Tax Avoidance?

Saving tax legally is known as tax avoidance. This is simply arranging your affairs so that the law has a smaller claim on your pocket than it would if you did things differently. Tax avoidance needs to be carefully distinguished from tax evasion, which is simply cheating the Inland Revenue by lies and deception. This is not allowed and if you do it you can end up in prison.

You should never allow the distinction between avoidance and evasion to become blurred because the consequences can be serious. The difference has been colourfully described as 'the thickness of a prison wall' and, as you will remember, Lester Piggott found this out the hard way. He was not the first person to evade tax and find himself in prison – and he will not be the last. If you are in any doubt, consider your course of action carefully and objectively, and if you are still in doubt seek professional advice. A good professional adviser should be able to explain how you can do what you would like to do without crossing the line into illegality.

Morality is a more difficult question. It is said that there is no morality, or indeed any equity, in tax, but this means either that you cannot be made to pay tax because of some high-sounding moral principle or that you cannot be relieved from paying tax for the same reason. Your liability depends on the law, not on some ill-defined moral code. But that is only half the story. Although your tax liability has nothing to do with morality, your conduct assuredly has. You should always conduct your tax affairs in a moral and honourable fashion – anything less is likely to lead to dishonesty and this can quickly become evasion and lead to a lot of trouble.

The conclusion from all this is that tax has to be paid because the law says so; if the law does not say so, you don't pay. In principle it is as simple as that.

A bit of Lateral Thinking

So you have to work within the rules to save the tax and often it is just a matter of some lateral thinking. To give you an extremely simple example, say a packet of 20 cigarettes carries a tax of 50p but packets of 10 cigarettes carry a tax of only 20p, you avoid 10p tax by buying two packets of 10 instead of one packet of 20.

It can become more complicated. The rule might be that if you buy two packets of 10 at the same time you are deemed to be buying a packet of 20 and you pay the higher tax. So maybe you buy 10 now and 10 later.

6

Again the rule might be that sales of cigarettes to the same person during a certain period of time have to be aggregated. So that would not work. You could therefore buy 10 from one shop and 10 from another – or possibly you could buy 18 from a vending machine. Alternatively, you could ask your wife to buy some for you, or have them sent here from abroad – and so it goes on.

The basic message is that when you know the basis on which the tax is imposed you can arrange things so that you fall outside it. So, if you know the rules, you are in with a chance.

Inland Revenue Practices

Everybody knows that there is always a distinction between law and practice and nowhere is this more true than in the collection of taxes. The Inland Revenue have published hundreds of practices about how they will deal with various tax matters and there are hundreds more unpublished practices. It is essential always to remember that the Inland Revenue is only entitled to your money if the law says so. They might have a convenient practice, but that cannot go further than the law allows. Accordingly, every published practice carries a bold statement that it does not affect your legal rights, so if you do not agree with it you can always have the matter dealt with on a strictly legal basis.

There are some additional practices which are known as extra statutory concessions whereby, quite simply and overtly, the Inland Revenue does not charge tax which it knows should properly be levied. Usually the reason is that the strict rules give rise to a result which they did not intend and which they want to alleviate. They could ask the government to change the law, but it could be extremely complicated to do so, so they just say that in certain cases they will not charge the tax. There are a large number of these concessions and they are published in a free booklet – IR1 – available from all tax offices.

The existence of concessions is highly controversial, but nobody complains too much because concessions mean that you pay less tax than the law provides. However, it is generally thought to be a bad policy for the Inland Revenue to have such a discretion – in one case it was said by the judge that people should be taxed by the law and not untaxed by concession. Nevertheless, despite frequent judicial criticism they remain and will no doubt continue as a permanent feature of our tax system.

As far as you, the taxpayer, are concerned, these distinctions between law and practice are of no great significance – if you pay less tax because of a strict application of the law, or because of some practice or concession, you will be equally happy. So just having a knowledge of the tax rules will not be enough because if there *is* a published practice or concession which will relieve you of the tax, that is just as important.

It would be wrong to think that concessions and other practices are applied only at the whim of the Inland Revenue and cannot be relied on. Although they do not have the force of law, and you cannot be made to accept an extra statutory practice, you *can* force the Inland Revenue to apply it for your benefit. Our system of administrative law requires government bodies to abide by their published pronouncements and it is possible to take legal action against the Inland Revenue and insist that they apply it to you. Of course, they can withdraw the concession at any time, but what they cannot do is to deny the benefit of a concession to you and allow it to somebody else.

The procedure is complex and it is inappropriate to deal with it here, but the principle is well worth bearing in mind. Throughout this book concessions and practices will be highlighted where they provide a particular opportunity for tax saving.

An Important Case: *Furniss* v. *Dawson*

Whenever thoughts turn to tax saving, and particularly the exploitation of loopholes, whether intended or otherwise, one has to consider the important tax case of *Furniss* v. *Dawson*. This case, decided in 1981, was the culmination of a series of cases brought by the Inland Revenue to defeat the artificial exploitation of various reliefs and allowances provided by the tax rules. It represented the high-water mark in the Inland Revenue 'new approach' to tax avoidance, which started with a case known as *Ramsay*, and is sometimes referred to as the *Ramsay* doctrine. You should not start trying to avoid tax by exploiting loopholes without appreciating its existence.

This doctrine gives rise to the general principle that it is not enough just to rearrange your affairs in a way which gives you the lowest tax liability, if the steps you take to do so are artificial. That is not to say the steps are false or unreal; if that were the case the steps would be properly disregarded as shams and could be ignored altogether. The idea is that if you enter into a series of transactions which, although they look all right individually, when looked at as a whole really represent a single composite transaction undertaken purely for the purpose of saving tax, the Inland Revenue can in these circumstances look at the position at the beginning and at the end, and charge accordingly by ignoring the intermediate steps.

For example, if you were to transfer an asset to your wife which she then sells, taking advantage of various reliefs or exemptions available to her, and then she gives the sale proceeds back to you, the Inland Revenue could say that the whole arrangement was preordained. Namely, that the gift to your wife was just one step in the plan which had no purpose other than the avoidance of tax and they would regard the sale as being made by you.

Thankfully, in 1988, the opportunity for the Inland Revenue to adopt this line of reasoning was severely curtailed by another series of cases, the most important of these being *Craven* v. *White*. This case affirmed the validity of the *Ramsay* doctrine, but placed strict limitations on its use. It does not matter that the transactions are undertaken for the avoidance of tax; that is not enough for the Inland Revenue to challenge them under the *Ramsay* doctrine. For the Inland Revenue to apply the doctrine, not only must there be a preordained series of transactions and steps inserted which have no commercial purpose and without any likelihood that the preordained result will not take place, the following conditions must also apply:

- the intermediate steps must serve no other purpose than the saving of tax;
- all the steps must be preordained to a degree of certainty and the taxpayer must be in control over the result at the time that the intermediate steps are taken;
- there must be no interruption between the intermediate transactions and the disposal to the ultimate purchaser.

If all these conditions are satisfied, the Inland Revenue can ignore the intermediate steps and charge tax on that basis. In a capital gains tax context this will normally mean that the original owner of the asset would be treated as if he had sold the asset directly to the ultimate purchaser and will be taxed accordingly. So, the *Ramsay* doctrine can be regarded as merely a means of interpreting tax law and not the establishment of a new principle at all.

It will be apparent from this that what really matters is not *what* you do, but *how* you do it. Looking at the above conditions individually, you will see that the first way out of difficulty is to ensure that the intermediate steps do have a purpose beyond merely saving tax.

To take the simple example referred to above, you could reasonably divide the assets between you and your wife, so as to effect a more appropriate allocation of your wealth, to provide her with financial security or to give her some income of her own. One way of demonstrating the validity of this purpose is to ensure that your wife has the assets for a reasonable period and, if possible actually receives income from the assets. If a sale takes place your wife should keep the proceeds herself.

The second condition will obviously not apply unless all the steps are preordained, and this means more than just preconceived. It must be certain that the steps will all take place and the end result will be under the control of the taxpayer at the time. So if, for example, you are planning to sell some shares but you do not yet have a purchaser lined up – or even if you do, the purchaser would be free to withdraw from the transaction if he changed his mind – you would not be in any danger. Just arranging things so that you would be in a good tax position in the event that a sale were to take place is nothing like enough to enable the Inland Revenue to invoke the *Ramsay* doctrine.

The third condition is simply a matter of timing, so a significant delay between the various steps and the end result is likely to give the Inland Revenue some difficulty in trying to apply this approach.

I have given the above explanations at some length in order to emphasise the need for tax-saving arrangements to be undertaken with care, and preferably they should be planned well in advance. The ideas I refer to in this book need not fall foul of the *Ramsay* doctrine, but you must appreciate that if they are carried out hurriedly or carelessly, almost any tax planning arrangement could fall within its scope and thus be rendered ineffective.

Where are you Resident?

This book is mainly concerned with how tax can be saved by UK residents. People who are resident outside the UK are not generally chargeable to UK tax, except on their UK income, so you might consider going abroad for a while if by doing so you can escape a large tax liability. In later chapters there are numerous references to residence and non-residence for tax purposes and in order that these ideas can be properly understood I should explain briefly the concept of residence and ordinary residence.

Residence

There are three main tests for determining whether somebody is resident in the UK and you only have to satisfy one of them.

1. A person who is physically present in the UK for more than 183 days in the tax year will always be regarded as resident for that year. Days of departure and arrival are generally ignored for this purpose. Where physical presence in the UK is for less than 183 days, you cannot be resident under this test, but there may be another test which will cause you to be resident.

2. A person who visits the UK for an average of 3 months per annum for 4 consecutive years would be regarded as resident in the UK thereafter. However, if it is clear when he first visits the UK that his visits will average 3 months per annum for 4 years he will be regarded as resident from the outset.

3. Where a person has accommodation available for his use in this country he will be treated as resident here for any year in which he sets foot in the UK. Use or ownership of the accommodation is irrelevant; all that matters is that the accommodation is available for his use during his presence here – irrespective of whether it is convenient to occupy or even visit the accommodation. However, the existence of available accommodation can be ignored if the person works full-time abroad and performs no duties (or only incidental duties) in the UK.

Having looked at these tests you may decide that you can fall outside them, but you might still find yourself treated as taxable in the UK. For example, you might be outside the UK for the whole of a tax year, in which case you do not satisfy any of these tests.

Unfortunately, there is an additional condition which is that if you are physically absent from the UK for a whole tax year for the purpose only of 'occasional residence' abroad, that is for a temporary or perhaps an itinerant purpose in other countries, you will still be regarded as chargeable to tax in the UK as if you were resident. So, if you want to become non-resident by being away for a complete tax year you must make quite sure that you go somewhere specific, for a particular purpose and stay there.

Remember, too, that you can be treated as resident in two (or more) different countries at the same time.

Ordinary Residence

Ordinary residence has comparatively little relevance for income tax, but it is the main determinant for capital gains tax, so you do not avoid capital gains tax simply by becoming non-resident – you have to become not ordinarily resident as well.

Ordinary residence is a more difficult concept and one which is broadly equivalent to habitual residence. Ordinary residence does not require physical presence in the UK and it is therefore possible for a person to be resident in the UK (perhaps by virtue of the existence of available accommodation), but ordinarily resident somewhere else if he normally lives abroad. Similarly, it is quite possible for a person to be not resident in the UK by establishing residence in another country, but without losing his UK ordinary residence. However, it is not possible to be ordinarily resident in more than one country at the same time.

If you are planning to save some capital gains tax by becoming both not resident and not ordinarily resident, you will take a significant risk if you make your gain before the Inland Revenue have agreed, at least provisionally, that you are no longer ordinarily resident in the UK.

To have any chance of success you must be away for at least a complete tax year and preferably for the subsequent two years as well. When you eventually do come back to the UK, the Inland Revenue may review the position and decide whether they were right in treating you as non-resident on the earlier date; if they decide against you, and you have made a big capital gain during your absence, they will be rather keen to charge tax on the basis that you had not lost your ordinary residence at the time you made the gain. Beware! Long and expensive negotiations may ensue.

Domicile

The concept of domicile is entirely different from residence and ordinary residence, and is of enormous importance in connection with UK taxation because of the tax privileges which are given to individuals who are not UK domiciled. In broad terms, a non-UK-domiciled individual is chargeable to UK tax on his foreign income and chargeable gains only if the income or gains are actually brought to the UK – this is called taxation on the remittance basis.

If you have enough money in the UK to meet your living expenses you can, as a non-UK-domiciled person, keep all your savings abroad and pay no income tax or capital gains tax, unless you bring the money here. Indeed, in the chapters dealing with income tax it is explained how to arrange for the money to be brought here without any tax by using the specific wording of the remittance basis rules. Other provisions which confer equally valuable reliefs for inheritance tax are covered in Chapter 7.

There is a great deal of misunderstanding about the concept of domicile and in particular how you can get hold of a much more favourable domicile than the one you presently possess. The extent of the misunderstandings and the possible tax advantages that are available are so great that some detailed explanation of the rules is called for.

It is no surprise that because non-UK-domiciled individuals can live in the UK for substantial periods and pay no UK tax at all, many people try extremely hard to establish a foreign domicile. However, the Inland Revenue are equally aware of the advantages and are therefore rather reluctant to agree that a person is not UK domiciled without detailed enquiry. Unfortunately, however, a lack of knowledge about the details of the rule lead some people to take rather an optimistic view of the subject. It takes a great deal more than just buying a house abroad and living there for part of the year to establish a foreign domicile.

Domicile is not a term specifically defined for tax purposes, but takes its meaning from the general law. It is fair to say that a person is domiciled in the country which he regards as his natural home and where he intends to stay, or return to, permanently.

A domicile of origin is essentially the domicile you were born with; usually it is determined by the domicile of your father at the time of your birth – where you were actually born has little or nothing to do with it. Accordingly, if you are claiming to have a foreign domicile of origin you must investigate the circumstances of your parents at the time of your birth and take into account what you have done and where you have lived since that date, particularly since the age of 16, which is the age when you are able to acquire an independent domicile.

The rule for the acquisition of a domicile of choice is simply stated thus: 'A person acquires a domicile of choice in a country by the combination of residence and the intention of permanent or indefinite residence but not otherwise.'

You will see immediately that you cannot possibly have a domicile of choice in a country unless you actually reside there – so you cannot claim a foreign domicile of choice unless you have at least established a permanent residence in that country.

Secondly, you have to show that you have an intention of permanent or indefinite residence in that other country. Intention is a subjective matter and it is therefore difficult to prove. It is not enough to say that you have the necessary intention – the Inland Revenue will require positive proof and an investigation into your personal circumstances will be necessary.

Establishing Foreign Connections

One point which is fatal to the claim for a domicile of choice in a foreign country is to have an intention of returning to the UK in the long term. If you do have such an intention you are sunk – and if you do ultimately return to the UK the Inland Revenue are most unlikely to accept that you ever acquired a domicile of choice while you were abroad. Any indication that you are retaining long-term connections with the UK will seriously damage your argument, and so will frequent visits here.

There is a popular myth that buying a burial plot in another country is all you need to do to establish a domicile of choice in that country. There is some underlying sense to that idea, but it is invariably overstated. If you are intended to be buried in a particular country it does give some indication that you have an intention of staying there until you die. But for the Revenue that is by no means enough – it is just one of the many factors to be taken into account.

So, if you want to stand any chance of saving UK tax by establishing a foreign domicile of choice you are going to have to live in that other country preferably in long-term (not rented) accommodation and to sever all continuing connections with the UK – and even then you will have to wait a long time. If you think you would be able to snatch the pot of gold by a mere cosmetic rearrangement of your affairs, think again.

Keeping your Foreign Domicile of Origin

If you *are* in the fortunate position of having a foreign domicile and you come and live in the UK, it is obviously desirable for you to retain your domicile of origin. There is a crucial distinction here between a person with a domicile of origin and a person with a domicile of choice. A domicile of origin is amazingly adhesive and will stay with you through thick and thin, unless you take positive steps to acquire a domicile of choice. You can leave your country of origin vowing never to return, but you will keep your domicile of origin unless and until you acquire a domicile of choice elsewhere by residing with the intention of permanent or indefinite residence in that country.

You will immediately see the contrast with the domicile of choice and the ease with which it can be abandoned. Furthermore, it should be recognised that if you have a domicile of choice which is abandoned, the most likely consequence is not that you acquire a new domicile of choice (which will inevitably take some time), but that your domicile of origin will revive.

What this means is that you can say what you like about your country of origin, but providing you do not have an intention to reside permanently in the UK you will keep your non-domiciled privileges. This means that you should take great care not to conduct yourself in a manner which indicates that you have in fact acquired a domicile of choice here.

=2=

GETTING DOWN TO BUSINESS

Preceding Year Basis of Assessment

If you run a business, or have any trading or professional income, it will be taxed under Schedule D; this contrasts with income from employment which is taxed under Schedule E. It is usually much more advantageous to be taxed under Schedule D as a self-employed person and this subject will be looked at in detail at the end of this chapter.

The way income tax is charged on trading and professional income gives rise to a real opportunity for tax saving, provided you plan correctly and understand how your taxable profits will be calculated. Generally, the tax is charged on the preceding year basis, that is to say on the profits made in the previous year. However, when a new business starts there is, of course, no profit in the preceding year, so you are charged tax on the profit in the first three years in the following manner.

Year 1: From the date of commencement to the following 5 April.

Year 2: The profit for the first 12 months of the business.

Year 3: The profit for the accounts for a 12-month period ending in the preceding year, but if there are no such accounts, the first 12 months' profit is again charged to tax.

This is the basic rule and you can use it to your advantage in a number of ways.

17

It may seem a bit tough to pay tax on your first 12 months' profit three times over, but don't worry; it will usually be exactly what you want because the profit for the first 12 months of any business is likely to be rather low. Even if it isn't, you can make arrangements to reduce your profits and save the tax three times over. If the profits are disproportionately low in the first 12 months you will pay very little tax and the same will obviously apply if these low profits are again taxed in the second and third years. Have a look at the example on page 21.

If for some reason it is inconvenient for the second and third years' profits to be taxed in this way you may ask the Inland Revenue for the assessments for those two years to be revised to the actual profits made in each year. When that happens, the fourth year will be based on the preceding year, i.e. the profits for the accounts ending in the third year. This obviously needs to be borne in mind in deciding whether an election for the actual basis for the second and third years will be worth while.

The final point to note is that you can choose your own accounting date and this can have the most enormous effect on the profits to be charged. Not only can it determine the amount of profit which is shown in the accounts, but it also enables you to determine which accounts or profits are taxed during the three years involved.

It will be obvious that the potential tax savings involved here are very substantial indeed, and a lot of thought and even more calculation will be required before you decide how the profits for the opening years are going to be taxed. The initiative is almost entirely on your side – and if you don't take advantage of it you only have yourself to blame.

For decades it has been suggested that the preceding year basis gives rise to so many problems that it ought to be scrapped and changed to an actual basis from start to finish. Such a change was made with the taxation of companies in 1965 which works quite satisfactorily, but no such change has been made to the taxation of individuals. However, a consultative document entitled 'A simpler system for taxing the self-employed' was issued on 14 August 1991, which indicates that a change is being seriously considered. Whether this will come about, and what form it will take is far from clear. For the moment the above opportunities are available and those who take the trouble to take advantage of them can save themselves large amounts of tax.

Choosing your Accounting Date

Anybody who has trading or professional income must prepare accounts regularly to submit to the tax authorities so that they can be properly taxed. If you fail to do this the Inland Revenue will guess what your profits were (usually it is a bad guess – and much too high) and charge tax accordingly. This encourages you to send in your accounts showing the real profit. If the Inland Revenue's guess is too low, they will charge penalties and interest on top of the tax when they find out the true profits, so it is usually better to send in your accounts on time.

The date to which you make up your accounts is entirely a matter for you – the Inland Revenue cannot interfere. It should therefore be carefully chosen not only to promote the best position for the opening years (and the closing years – see below), but also to achieve a number of other purposes.

Flow of Income

The first point to consider is the flow of income. If the income is the same every month there is not a lot of scope, but a new business will not usually be in that happy position. If your work is intermittent, the flow of income will also be variable and it is therefore advantageous to draw up your accounts to a date immediately before (and not immediately after) a large amount of income arises.

For example:
Assume that you started your business on 1 January 1991 and
the income for the first 12 months is like this:

March	1000
April	1000
May	1500
July	5000
September	2000
November	500
December	7000
	£18000

With these figures you would be well advised to choose an
accounting date of 11 months to 30 November. Your accounts
would then show profits of £11,000 instead of the £18,000
which would arise by choosing a 12-month accounting
period to 31 December. The first year's assessment will be
based on the profits from 1 January 1991 to 5 April 1991,
which is $3/11$ of the £11,000 profit to 30 November; this
amounts to £3,000 instead of $3/12$ of the profit of £18,000 to 31
December which would be £4,500.

In the second year you may think that the whole of the
£7,000 will be taxed so that the advantage is rather small.
However, that is most unlikely to be the case. Remember that
in your second year you will be taxed on the profits for the
first 12 months, but this is found by apportioning on a time
basis the profits shown in the accounts. Accordingly, the first
12 months will be made up of the accounts to 30 November
1991 plus $1/12$ of the following 12 months' accounts to 30
November 1992. Unless the profits for the year ended 30
November 1992 are £84,000 or more, $1/12$ is bound to be less
than £7,000 and there will be a further saving for the second
year and probably the third year as well. For example, if the
profit for the year ended 30 November 1992 was £40,000, the
first three years would be taxed like this:

1990/1 $^3/_{11}$ × £11,000		3000
1991/2 11 months to 30/11/91	11000	
$1^1/_2$ × £40,000	3333	
		14333
1992/3 first 12 months again		14333
Total *taxable* profits for first 3 years		**£31666**

However, if you had chosen a 31 December 1991 accounting date, the three years' assessments would be:

1990/1	$^3/_{12}$ × £18,000	4500
1991/2	Year ended 31/12/91	18000
1992/3	Year ended 31/12/91	18000
		£40500

So for the sake of choosing your accounting date one month earlier you would save tax on nearly £11,000.

Improve your Cash Flow

The second reason for thinking carefully about your accounting date is because it can substantially improve your cash flow. Tax is paid on trading and professional income in two instalments, on 1 January in the tax year and 1 July following the tax year. In the first three years it makes little difference, but once a business is on the preceding year basis it can be of significant advantage to have chosen an accounting date early in the tax year.

For example:
If you make up your accounts to 31 March each year, the profits for the year ended 31 March 1992 will be taxed in 1992/3 and the tax will be payable in two instalments on 1 January 1993 and 1 July 1993. Therefore, you have 9 months from the end of your accounts until the first instalment of tax needs to be paid.

21

However, if you were to choose a 30 April accounting date the position is much better. The profits for the year ended 30 April 1992 will be taxed in 1993/4 and the first instalment of the tax will not be payable until 1 January 1994. So, a one-month difference in choosing your accounting date gives you a whole year's extra time-lag before having to pay the tax.

In terms of cash flow this is obviously extremely valuable – you have a whole extra year to work out your tax bill and save up for it.

Accounting For Your Profit

If you are in business or have professional income, accounts will need to be prepared for your selected accounting period and submitted to the Inland Revenue. In many cases this will be dealt with by your accountant. If you also understand and appreciate the methods by which profits can be calculated, to the extent that any variation is possible, you will be in a better position to arrange things to your advantage. It would obviously be better for the variation to be downwards rather than up-wards. The lower the profits, of course, the less tax you will pay.

We have already seen that by a judicious choice of accounting date it is possible to defer some income to a subsequent period. However, there are limits to what you can do. Accounts are usually prepared on what is known as the 'bills delivered' basis, so that you bring into account all the amounts for which you have issued an invoice during the period, whether or not they have been paid. It is possible in some cases to prepare accounts on the 'cash received' basis so you only bring amounts into account when you have received the money; however, the Inland Revenue are hostile to this method and you will not easily be able to adopt this basis (and avoid some of its adverse implications) without professional help.

It is therefore possible to reduce your profits for a year simply by deferring the issue of invoices until after the end of your accounting period. It is for you to decide when to send out your bills, not the Inland Revenue, and they cannot insist that you issue invoices at any particular time. In any business, especially one which involves buying and selling goods, deferring the issue of an invoice when the goods have already been delivered may not be effective anyway. A short delay in issuing your invoices is unlikely to excite the Inland Revenue, but if your Inspector of Taxes feels that you are abusing the position, he could well argue that the sales should be brought into account anyway. He could say that when you delivered the goods to the customer in accordance with his order (and assuming that the goods are not defective), the contract was then complete and the sale had been made. The sale should therefore be brought into your accounts, even though you had not issued an invoice.

You should, however, bear in mind that you are unlikely to be paid until you send your customers a bill, so it might not always be a desirable course of action. Furthermore, the bank manager will have a particular interest in your accounts and he may not be impressed if you end up with low profits; he may start making unpleasant noises about your overdraft. You need to adopt a sensible course and simply avoid a great rush of bills at your year end. If you are in a seasonal business where there will always be a high volume of activity at your year end, choose an accounting date a little earlier than that to avoid the rush.

Work in Progress

It is also worth while to consider the question of 'work in progress' – that is work which you have done during the year but which you have not yet billed out. This can often be a substantial amount and the Inland Revenue sometimes want you to bring a figure for work in progress into your accounts. It is a perfectly reasonable accounting policy to do so and it does reflect more properly the profit made by your business during the year.

However, work in progress is notoriously difficult to value. Half-completed work may have no value at all, and in any event the value of the work in progress may not exceed the costs you have incurred in doing it. You can add to these costs a proportion of attributable overheads if you want to (or leave it out if you prefer), but you cannot include any element of profit, except in very special cases involving long-term contracts. If you are a professional person, most of the value of your work will be your own time or the time of your partners and that is not a cost. If you exclude the proprietors' or partners' time, the work in progress is usually negligible and no problem is likely to arise with the Inland Revenue.

Trading Stock

The value of the trading stock may be another important element in determining the profit. In broad terms, the higher the value of the stock, the higher will be your profit (and vice versa); for this reason the Inland Revenue are rather interested in stock values.

The proper basis of valuing stock is cost, or net realisable value if that is lower. It is perfectly in order to examine your stock carefully and to write down the value of old or slow-moving stock on the basis that you may not get much for it. However, subsequent events will usually show whether that judgement was reasonable – and remember that the Inland Revenue are always looking at these things with the benefit of hindsight. A general writing down of the stock without any reasonable justification is therefore unlikely to be effective. It should also be remembered that a low closing stock will increase the profits for the subsequent year and that must always be taken into account.

When a Business Ceases . . .

It may be thought that it is unfair to pay tax on one year's profits two or three times over because this could mean that over the lifetime of a business tax will be charged on more than the profits actually made by the business. Fortunately, there are some corresponding provisions in the closing years of a business and this gives rise to a substantial opportunity for advantage, even better than that which exists in its opening years.

When a business ceases, the basis of assessment goes into reverse. The assessment for the final tax year, that is to say the tax year in which the business ceased, is based on the profit from the previous 5 April to the date of cessation. However, the assessment for that year was going to be based on the profits for the preceding year, so what happens to those profits? The answer is that they do not get taxed at all. This may seem surprising but it is simply the corollary to the position in the opening years when the first 12 months' profits are taxed more than once. But just as you have the opportunity to elect for the second and third years to be taxed on the actual basis, the Inland Revenue has the same option in the two years preceding the cessation, if it would be to their advantage.

This often gives rise to a misunderstanding that, when a business ceases, the assessments for the earlier years are increased and you pay more tax. This conclusion is not necessarily correct. It is true that assessments for the two years preceding cessation may increase, but another year (and possibly two) will always drop out and will never be charged to tax.

This technique whereby you arrange for profits to fall out of assessment, is known, not surprisingly, as a 'drop-out' plan. Let's look at a business which illustrates all the above points.

For example:

Business starts 1 June 1989.

Profits for 11 months to 30 April 1990	15000
12 months to 30 April 1991	24000
to 30 April 1992	30000
30 April 1993	50000
30 April 1994	60000
30 April 1995	80000
Business ends on 31 May 1995 (1 month)	15000
	£274000

Assessments:

1989/90	1 June 1989 to 5 April 1990		
	$^{10}/_{11}$ × 15,000		13636
1990/1	1st 12 months to 31 May 1990		
	11 months to 30 April 1990	15000	
	$^{1}/_{12}$ × year ended 30 April 1991	2000	17000
1991/2	1st 12 months again		17000
1992/3	Year ended 30 April 1991		24000
1993/4	Year ended 30 April 1992		30000
1994/5	Year ended 30 April 1993		50000
1995/6	(final year) 6 April 1995 to		
	31 May 1995		
	$^{1}/_{12}$ × 80,000	6666	
	1 month to 31 May 1995	15000	21666
			£173302

What has happened here is that although the business has made profits of £274,000 over the period, it has been taxed only on £173,302: over £100,000 of profit has disappeared. Unfortunately, however, in these circumstances the Inland Revenue will certainly revise the assessments for the two years prior to cessation to the actual basis. In this example the years capable of adjustment by the Inland Revenue are 1993/4 and 1994/5, because on the preceding year basis profits of £30,000 and £50,000 would be taxed. If they adopt the actual basis for these years the figures look like this:

1993/4	Year ended 5 April 1994		
	$^{11}/_{12}$ × 30 April 1994	55000	
	$^{1}/_{12}$ × 30 April 1993	4167	59167
1994/5	Year ended 5 April 1995		
	$^{11}/_{12}$ × 30 April 1995	73333	
	$^{1}/_{12}$ × 30 April 1994	5000	78333
			137500

So the assessments for these two years are uplifted to the actual basis and an extra £57,500 is charged to tax. However, this increases the total assessments for the whole period to £230,802 which is still £43,000 lower than the actual profits for the whole period. This is because, although the 1994 and 1995 profits have been revised to actual, some of the 1992 and 1993 profits have escaped tax.

You will immediately appreciate that if you had done your drop-out plan correctly, you would make sure that the profits for 1992 and 1993 were the same as those for 1994 and 1995, so that even if the Inland Revenue were to exercise their option, it would not increase the overall amount of profits chargeable to tax.

Alternatively, you could change everything by arranging to cease business on 31 March 1995 instead of 31 May 1995. This changes the tax year in which you cease and therefore the years which are capable of adjustment by the Inland Revenue. You are able to cease your business at anyy time you choose, so you can work out all the figures in advance and arrange to cease the business at the most advantageous time.

How to Take Advantage of the Closing Provisions Without Actually Closing Your Business

It may be that your business is successful and you have no plans to cease trading, but you would still like to take advantage of the above rules to avoid tax on one or two years of profits. One of the ways of doing so would be to transfer your business to a company; your business would then cease and the company would start to carry on a new business. This would enable you to continue with the business, while at the same time gaining the advantage of a drop out. The whole subject of incorporation of a business is explained in detail in Chapter 3.

As an alternative you could go into partnership with another person. That would have the same effect because your business would still cease (and you would secure the drop out) and the partnership would commence a new business. If you want, you

27

can make an election for the partnership to be treated as carrying on a continuing trade, in which case the cessation would be deemed not to occur. However, you obviously would not make such an election of you wanted to create a cessation and a drop out.

The use of partnerships in this way is not always recommended, however, because there is a sting in the tail. The Inland Revenue got fed up with partnerships (particularly firms of accountants) contriving a cessation every 5 or 6 years because every time they did so a large amount of their profits fell out of assessment. The rules were therefore changed so that where a business is treated as ceasing by the introduction or retirement of a partner, the opening years of the new business are taxed on the actual basis for the next 4 years. This means that you can get your drop out once, but you then have to wait a long time before you can do it again. Furthermore, the 4-year actual basis period takes most of the advantage out of the drop out because it means higher tax assessments for the next 4 years.

The Advantages of Introducing A Partner

I have already explained that by introducing a partner, a cessation of the trade is deemed to occur and sometimes that is exactly what you want in order to create the appropriate 'drop out'. However, there is another advantage which can arise if you do not wish at the moment to create a cessation. It is possible for an election to be signed by both parties so that the deemed cessation does not take place, but the business is treated as continuing unchanged. This can have a substantial one-off tax advantage in the year of admission, because of the peculiarities of the preceding year basis of assessment.

For example:
Let us assume that you make up your accounts to 30 March each year and, for the year ended 31 March 1992, your profit was £50,000. You have an employee who was paid £20,000

during that year. If you bring him into partnership on 1 April 1992 and everything else remains the same, you can expect your profits for the year ended 31 March 1993 to be £70,000 because his earnings will no longer be a salary to an employee; because he is a partner, his earnings will now be part of the overall partnership profits. However, the profits assessed to tax for 1992/3 will be those for the year ended 31 March 1992, i.e. £50,000, and if his share of profit is still £20,000, your taxable income is reduced to only £30,000. (If you had a 30 April accounting date, this advantage would last for 2 years because the profits for 30 April 1991 would be taxed in 1992/3, and the profits for the year ended 30 April 1992 would be taxed in 1993/4).

You might therefore think it worth while to increase the salary of your employee for his final year of employment rather than to enhance his earnings on becoming a partner in order to increase the benefit of the tax deduction.

Dealing With Business Losses

If you are in business as a sole trader or partnership you may hit hard times and make a loss. This is serious because not only have you worked for a whole year for nothing, but you also end up with less than you started. You may think that if you make a loss, the last of your problems is likely to be tax, but although you do not have to pay tax if you make a loss, you may still have an outstanding tax bill on last year's profits and no money with which to pay it. In the circumstances you will need to ensure that you get every penny of benefit from making a loss.

Don't be taken in by people who talk about running their business at a tax loss as if it were some kind of advantage. If you make a loss you have lost money and even if you can obtain full tax relief for the loss you will still recover only 40 per cent of it. However, it is possible to make a loss *for tax purposes* when you actually make a real profit, and this is a wholly different matter!

Forwards, Backwards and Sideways

When a loss arises you must make sure that it is relieved in the most advantageous way, which means getting the most tax relief you can for it. The main relief is to set the loss against any other income you have on which you pay tax. Usually it is necessary to make a claim within 2 years of the end of the tax year in which the loss was made, and you can thereby obtain a repayment of the tax you have paid on other income.

However, that is only the beginning because you have a lot of opportunities open to you and the option you should take is the one which gives you the maximum tax repayment. It is obviously much better to set the loss against income which is being taxed at 40 per cent rather than income which is being taxed at 25 per cent, and this is where you need to consider your options carefully.

Your first option is simply to carry forward the loss against the future profits of the same trade, and although there is no time limit by which the losses have to be used, the relief is only available against profits for the same trade – not some other trade. So if your business may be coming to an end you must claim relief elsewhere, because when the trade ceases the possibility of relief for the loss will be forfeited.

If the loss is made in the first 3 years of a new trade you are able to carry back the loss for 3 years against your other income, with relief being given against latest years first.

Where a loss arises after you have been trading for more than 3 years, you can set off the loss against the profits which are being taxed in the year in which the loss is being made by reason of the preceding year basis. For example, if you have a loss for the year ended 31 March 1992, that is to say the tax year 1991/2, you can deduct the loss against the profits for the year ended 31 March 1991, which would otherwise be taxed in the year 1991/2. This will reduce the amount of tax you pay on 1 January 1992 and 1 July 1992. If, therefore, you know you are going to make a loss you can write to the Inland Revenue and ask them to postpone the January tax payment until your losses are agreed and this can be very helpful with your cash flow. However, it is important to get it right, because if you guess wrong interest will run on the tax unpaid. If you did not make much profit last year either, you can set the loss against any other income which has been taxed during 1991/2.

Alternatively, you can leave the previous year alone and set the loss against your other income for the following year 1992/3, the year in which you would have been taxed, had you made a profit for the year ended 31 March 1992. If you do that you will obviously have to wait for your relief, although if you have a job and are taxed under PAYE you could ask for your code number to be adjusted so as to enable loss relief to be given month by month by a reduction in your PAYE deductions. You may feel that it is not particularly helpful to claim relief in this way when you can obtain a tax repayment in respect of the previous year, but it will make a lot of sense if you were only paying 25 per cent on last year's profits, but will be paying tax at 40 per cent next year. It would then clearly make sense not to carry the loss back, but to use it against the following year and obtain a larger tax repayment. The delay will obviously be worth while, but note that you should take repayment supplement into account (see below).

To conclude this chronological sequence, if you make a loss in your final year of trading you obviously cannot carry it forward – there will be no profits of the same trade for it to be set against. However, there is a further relief known as 'terminal loss' relief which enables you to carry back the loss to be set against profits of the trade for the last 3 years, in a rather similar manner to the way in which relief is given in the opening 3 years.

Although you can pick and choose the type of relief you want, I'm afraid you cannot split the loss and carry a bit forward, a bit back and a bit sideways to mop up income taxed at the highest rates only. You must claim the whole of the relief in one way, and only if that is not sufficient to use up all the losses can you relieve them somewhere else.

Capital Gains Relief

If all this does not help you there is another opportunity, which is to set the loss against any capital gains you make in the same or the following year. You may think that this is rather unlikely because you are hardly going to be making substantial capital gains, at least sufficient to exhaust your capital gains tax exemption, if you are making a loss. However, you may have some shares and other savings which you need to sell to keep the business afloat or to meet your living expenses – if you are making a loss you certainly have no income coming in.

Alternatively, you may simply take the opportunity to sell some of your shares by a bed and breakfast operation to create a tax-free gain to uplift your base value when you later come to dispose of the investments (see page 113). A bed and breakfast operation is usually done each year to make sure that the annual exemption is utilised, but if you have a loss which may not otherwise be relieved you could use it against gains created by a bed and breakfast operation, so as to reduce your capital gains tax when you sell the investments in due course.

Another possibility is that your spouse may have some investments on which she could make a gain. Unfortunately, you cannot set your trading losses against her capital gains, but what she could do is to give you some of her investments (transfers between husbands and wives are effectively ignored for capital gains tax), so that you can sell them in order to make the gain against which you can relieve your loss. The gift must be genuine or the Inland Revenue will ignore it, so you will need to keep the proceeds of sale to demonstrate that the gift was real.

This brief summary of the options available shows what you can do with a trading loss and clearly some careful planning is necessary to get the best value for the loss. However, it is equally important to see what you can do with the rules to make them work even more to your advantage.

Using your Spouse's Allowances

One of the side-effects of the introduction of independent taxation is that a loss made by one spouse cannot any longer be set against the income of the other spouse. So this might be a good reason for being in partnership with your wife (there are other reasons for this which are dealt with in Chapter 5). If your spouse has other income which is taxed and she is a partner in your business as well, she will be entitled to her own share of the loss against her other income and will have the whole range of options available to her.

If you are not already in partnership with your wife you might find it attractive to bring her into partnership at the right time, because if you do you will have the opportunity to change the basis upon which you are charged to tax. The effect of this on the preceding year basis has already been explained, but in the context of loss relief you can secure a different advantage.

For example:

Let's say that you have made a loss which you would like to carry back 2 years. Last year you may not have made much profit, but the year before you made a good profit and paid tax at 40 per cent. Unfortunately, you cannot carry back the loss for 2 years so you are stuck. However, if you bring your wife (or anybody else for that matter) into partnership with you this will be treated as a cessation of the trade, so you can claim terminal loss relief and carry back the loss up to 3 years.

You do not *have* to do so – you can elect for the trade to continue by a 'continuance election', but the opportunity is there to claim terminal loss relief if it would be helpful in your circumstances.

Capital Allowances

Another area of flexibility arises with capital allowances. In your business you will have capital assets such as furniture and fittings, typewriters, computers and all sorts of office equipment, and you will receive capital allowances on these items at 25 per cent per annum on the reducing balance. Claims to capital allowances can create a loss or can augment an existing loss to maximise the loss relief available.

However, it may be that claiming these allowances does not do you much good in the year you would normally claim them. They may augment your loss, but if you would be stuck with relief at only 25 per cent, or worse still, you have made a small profit which is covered by your personal allowances, a claim for capital allowances to reduce a profit which will not be taxed anyway, would be a complete waste. You have an opportunity to disclaim your allowances. This does not mean that you lose them, because the expenditure on which they will be given would be undiminished for the following year. So by disclaiming your allowances for one year you increase the allowances for the nnext year, by which time you may have a greater range of opportunities available to you.

Additional Relief on Incorporation of a Business

In Chapter 3 you will see how a business can be transferred to a company in exchange for shares. It is unlikely that a business which consistently makes a loss would be transferred to a company, but it is possible that in the final year of trading a loss will arise. This may be a genuine trading loss or it may be created by a low stock transfer value or capital allowances, but in any event it will rank as a terminal loss and eligible for relief against the preceding 3 years. There are no provisions to allow the losses of the trade to be carried forward for relief against the company's profits.

However, there is another relief which allows a trader to claim relief for his loss against any income he derives from the company in later years, for example by way of salary or dividends. The relief is given against earned income in priority to unearned income, but the individual must be the beneficial owner of the company shares throughout the year of assessment for which the claim is made.

In practice the Inland Revenue will allow the relief, provided that the trader has not disposed of more than 20 per cent of the shares he received for the transfer.

This relief needs careful calculation, particularly in years where the rates of tax change; if the rates of tax increase it will obviously be much better to claim relief in this way, rather than carry back the losses by a terminal relief claim.

Interest from the Inland Revenue

One happy incident of loss relief and the tax-free payment which arises is the opportunity to obtain 'repayment supplement', which is what the Inland Revenue call interest when they pay it to you. Not only is it deeply satisfying when you receive interest from the Inland Revenue, it is also extremely valuable because it is paid at a reasonable rate and is tax free. The rate is variable, but it is the same rate that the Inland Revenue charge you on unpaid tax, so it is never too low. Unfortunately, the rules which apply for obtaining repayment supplement are much stricter than those for charging interest on unpaid tax but, provided you know the rules, you can use them to your advantage.

Generally, you do not become entitled to repayment supplement until 1 year after the end of the year of assessment to which the tax relates or from the 6 April following the date of payment of the tax. Where a loss arises and you are considering your options, you should also consider the incidence of repayment supplement. If, for example, you can set off your loss against other income for previous years, the addition of supplement can make it very much more worth while then carrying the loss forward.

If funds permit you can generate repayment supplement by carefully considering the dates on which you pay your tax. If you receive an assessment for a previous year, e.g., if the Inland Revenue are late in issuing the assessment and you know that it is excessive or that the income charged will be covered by loss relief, you can still make a payment of tax shown on the assessment (or more if you like) and interest will run on this overpayment from the reckonable date (which in these circumstances would be the following 5 April) until the 5th of the month following the date of repayment. When you get round to claiming your loss (and you will have 2 years in which to do this), you will have earned 2 years of tax-free repayment supplement, which is obviously extremely rewarding.

Being Self-Employed

I have already drawn your attention to the numerous advantages and loopholes which exist for the self-employed. In fact, this chapter has mainly been concerned with people who are in business on their own account, which is what being self-employed is all about. It is important to understand what constitutes self-employment and how you can secure treatment as a self-employed person. If you can be self-employed you need to know how to go about it and the conditions which need to be satisfied. But bear in mind that self-employment is not all roses. If you are in business on your own, you have no security of employment and although when things are going well it may seem little different from being an employee, when things start to go wrong the differences become painfully apparent. If the work you do is poor you may not even be paid and you may not get any other work either. There is no redundancy, salary in lieu of notice or holiday pay.

However, the self-employed are able to claim more expenses than employees. That is hardly surprising because they have to incur more expenses; nobody supplies them with a desk, a pen or paper, or even a cup of coffee – they have to buy all these things themselves. The rule relating to the deduction of expenses is that the expenditure has to be *wholly and exclusively* incurred for the purpose of the business. This is not as strict as the rule for employees where you can hardly claim for anything (as we will see in Chapter 3), but still, wholly and exclusively means what it says – there can be no private or personal element in the expenditure, or it will all be disallowed.

The Inspector of Taxes will usually allow a proportion of some expenses, such as the cost of running your home (if you work from home) and part of your telephone bills. You may also be able to pay a salary to your wife to take advantage of her allowances, and obtain tax relief for part of the expenses of running your car.

I do not propose to go through all the expenses which you might claim, as these can be found in any tax saving guide. However, at least part of the following can usually be allowed by negotiation with the Inland Revenue, either as a direct deduction from your profits or by way of an allowance for capital expenditure, provided of course that you can show a reasonable business purpose for the expenditure:

a) Cost of all materials used in the course of and preparation of your work.

b) The cost of typewriting and secretarial assistance. If this or other help is obtained from your spouse, it is entirely proper for a deduction to be claimed for the amounts paid for the work. The amounts claimed must actually be paid, and should be at the market rate, although an uplift can be made for unsocial hours etc. Payments to the spouse are of course taxable in their hands, and should therefore be most carefully considered. (See chapter 5 so that you do not inadvertently increase your overall tax liability.)

c) All expenditure on normal business items, such as postage, printing, stationery, professional and technical journals, periodicals, subscriptions to professional bodies. Books which are relevant to your work will be allowed, including a subscription to a book club if it would be helpful to you in obtaining books for your work.

d) The cost of business telephone calls and a proportion of the rental costs.

e) The cost of daily papers if they form part of your research material.

f) The cost of your personal computer, associated software, answering machine and fax.

g) TV, video recorder, CD and tape players can be eligible for a tax deduction where they are relevant to your work.

h) A proportion of the costs of your home such as lighting, heating, cleaning, rates (but not the personal Community Charge) if you carry on part of your work from your home. See also chapter 6 for the capital gains tax implications of making such a claim.

i) Expenditure on a desk, cabinets and other furniture and fittings to be used for business purposes.

j) Travelling and hotel expenses in connection with your work (see later).

k) The appropriate business proportion of your motor running expenses may also be claimed, although what is an appropriate proportion will depend upon your own particular circumstances; it is important to appreciate that the scale benefits, where you are taxed according to the size and cost of your car, do not apply to self-employed persons.

l) If a separate business bank account is maintained, any overdraft interest will be an allowable expense. This is the only circumstance in which overdraft interest is allowed for tax purposes, and care should be taken to avoid overdrafts in all other circumstances.

m) If you have any bad debts where a customer will not or cannot pay for your work, you can claim a tax deduction for the amount, provided you had already sent him an invoice which had been included in your accounts as income.

n) Visits to theatres and cinemas for research purposes, but not the amount relating to any guests. Unfortunately, expenditure on all types of business entertaining is specially denied relief; however, you can claim the cost of entertaining your own staff.

o) Agents' fees where appropriate and accountancy charges for dealing with your accounts each year.

p) Special clothing which you may need for your work, but not ordinary clothing which you wear for private purposes.

q) Half of any class 4 national insurance contributions.

There are bound to be many other items you could claim which will depend upon your precise circumstances and the nature of your work (such as the costs of a guard dog if you genuinely need one for security of your premises), and you should always have a valid reason before making your claim. You cannot expect to obtain full relief for everything because of the principle of duality of purpose, but if you put forward a reasonable case to the Inspector of Taxes he will usually allow at least a proportion of the expenditure.

Self-employment and Travelling Expenses

Travelling expenses to and from work are *not* allowable. Whether you like it or not, that is the rule. However, if you work from home you will never be travelling to and from work; you will always be travelling on business, because you start off from your place of work. If you go to a client's office to work you must make sure that you do not set up camp there for a lengthy period or the Inland Revenue will regard you as having your working base at that office. Make sure that you do some of the work at home so that you can protect your travelling expenses deduction.

If you are fortunate enough to find an assignment somewhere rather agreeable, for example in Cannes because you feel attendance at the film festival would be of untold benefit to your professional work, you should be aware that if you add a holiday to the end of your assignment the Inland Revenue may disallow the whole cost of the trip. They will say that the trip had a private as well as a business purpose, and therefore none of the costs will be allowed. However, if you arrive a day or two early to acclimatise yourself and leave a day or two later to avoid the rush you could achieve the same objective. But you must be able to say truthfully, when the Inland Revenue asks, that your purpose in going there was wholly and exclusively for your work, and you did not go for any other purpose. You cannot help it if the film festival is held in such a nice place and just because you enjoy it, you should not be denied a tax deduction. What would be fatal to your claim is if you were to go there intending to have a bit of a holiday at the same time.

Self-employed or Employee?

Difficulties will always arise in connection with those activities which can just as easily be undertaken as a self-employed person or as an employee. For example, if you are a journalist you can be employed by a newspaper or you can be freelance. If you work regularly for the same publication you may be able to enjoy most of the advantages of being an employee (other than job security and the related benefits), but still enjoy the tax advantages of being self-employed. The Inland Revenue are naturally rather keen to classify people as employees whenever they can, since they receive more tax that way, so you need to consider the tests of self-employment to see how you can adjust your circumstances to qualify for self-employed treatment.

The essential characteristic of an employee is that he is the servant of his employer. It is this master/servant relationship which is crucial in determining whether you are employed or self-employed. However, there is no single test which can be applied to determine whether you are employed or self-employed nor, unfortunately, is there an exhaustive list; furthermore there are no strict rules about how much weight should be given to one factor as against another. This may sound rather vague, but it is not nearly as imprecise as it seems. What you have to do is to look at all the relevant criteria and make a judgement about which side of the line your circumstances fall.

All the factors need to be weighed in the balance and you need to ensure that more of the factors indicate self-employment than otherwise. The main tests are as follows.

1. Whether the person for whom you work is able to control what you do and when you do it. You will no doubt want to do what he requires, but that is not necessarily the same thing.

2. Whether you are working exclusively for one person. If you are, this will be more consistent with an employment and will enhance the control he has over you. So, wherever possible, you should work for as many different people as you can and make quite sure that you are subject to no prohibitions on working elsewhere.

3. How you and the person for whom you work understand your relationship. If you both make it clear that you do not have a master/servant relationship (and you know what that means), it will be difficult for the Inland Revenue to argue that such a relationship exists. After all, it will be a question of contract. There are limits to which the Inland Revenue can look at your contract and add in a few terms, which neither of you intended, just to improve their argument. But if your relationship is in truth one of master and servant, just saying that it is not will hardly affect the position.

4. How you are paid. If you are paid a regular sum irrespective of the work actually undertaken, this looks rather like wages or a salary. You should register for VAT if your earnings reach the appropriate level and issue regular invoices for the specific work undertaken. If you are paid expenses these should be separately identified on your invoices.

5. Your place of work. If you work at your client's premises all the time you will be under greater control and no doubt there will be a higher degree of exclusivity; you will therefore acquire many of the characteristics of an employee. You

should do as much as possible of your work from your home or from your own office.

6. The provision of equipment. If you are provided with equipment for your work just like an employee, this may indicate that you are quite likely to be an employee. By all means use your client's equipment, but you should have some of your own as well.

7. Whether you must do the work yourself or whether you can arrange for the work to be done by others. This is not always possible because you may well have been engaged for your personal skills, but you should not be prohibited (e.g. in times of holiday and sickness) from being able to have the work performed by another person, providing, of course, that it is done to the appropriate standard.

8. The terms of your contract. This will obviously give a clear indication of your working relationship and you should be very careful not to include any terms which are inconsistent with being self-employed. You may think this will be difficult, but if you want all the benefits of being an employed person, and you put such things in the contract, you may end up being treated as one. Very careful drafting of the contract is required. If you are in doubt just think what sort of contract you might draw up between yourself and your solicitor or your accountant for work to be done on your behalf. This will give you a good guide to the type of terms which ought to be included and those which are clearly inappropriate.

If you can satisfy all these tests you will be able to sustain self-employed treatment and gain the advantages which go with it, but you should always remember that your contract and the manner in which you conduct your work may well be enquired into in some detail by the Inland Revenue. Never work on the principle that 'This will do'; it will probably do very nicely for the Inland Revenue.

From the Employer's Point of View

It is not always the person doing the work who wants to be self-employed. It is often the employer who wants the person doing the work to be self-employed. He may well not want all the obligations and aggravation of having employees, nor indeed the costs of national insurance contributions, which can be considerable. The employer's position is much worse because it is he who takes all the risk. If he engages somebody to do some work on a self-employed basis, but the other person is not really self-employed (he just agrees to call himself self-employed because it would be advantageous for tax purposes for both of them), the employer could end up with a huge bill. It is the employer who is liable to deduct PAYE and NIC and pay it over to the Inland Revenue and it is he who will be pursued by the Inland Revenue to pay these amounts if he has failed to do so.

It is a foolish employer who pays his workers on a self-employed basis without having really good grounds for thinking that they are genuinely self-employed.

LOOPHOLES IN BUSINESS TAXATION

Incorporating a Business

In this section we will be looking into the advantages which can be contrived by transferring a business to a company. This is a complex area and not all the implications can be covered here. In any event a detailed explanation is inappropriate because what really matters is where you can find the loopholes.

When to Incorporate

When you start a business it is obviously important to decide whether you should trade on your own as a sole trader, or perhaps in a partnership, or whether you should incorporate a company, and this can be a most difficult judgement. Given the wide variety of possible circumstances, there is no general rule which enables you to say which would be the best route. Every case will be different and there will be commercial considerations to take into account.

However, in many cases it will be preferable to start the business as a sole trader or partnership, and for the business to be transferred to a company at a later date. This will enable a 'drop out' to be obtained so that part of the business profits are not taxed, as well as ensuring that tax on future profits can be limited to corporation tax at a flat rate of 25 per cent. Other income tax advantages can be contrived, and there will be an opportunity to save capital gains and inheritance tax.

Working Abroad

One area where the incorporation of a business can lead to a substantial advantage (beyond those otherwise referred to in this chapter) is when an individual expects to work overseas for a significant part of each year. In such circumstances that individual would continue to be chargeable to income tax on the whole of his worldwide earnings as a self-employed person. However, if he were to transfer the business to a company, and become employed by the company, he would be able to plan the pattern of his foreign trips in such a way that his foreign earnings could be free of tax by satisfying the requirements for the 100 per cent deduction. The operation of the 100 per cent deduction, and the other advantages which can be obtained from working abroad, are explained in detail later in this chapter.

Choosing the Right Method of Transfer

In practical terms there are two main methods of incorporating a business and the method chosen will depend upon what is intended to be achieved by incorporation. The methods are:

1. transferring all the assets of the business to a company and arranging for the company to take over some or all of the business liabilities;

2. transferring the business as a going concern to a company in exchange for shares in the company or for a combination of shares and cash.

The meaning of 'business' in this connection is obviously of great importance. The term 'business' is wider than 'trade' and, although the Inland Revenue regard a business as an activity in the nature of a trade, this seems an unnecessarily restrictive interpretation. There is some support for the idea that the letting of property can represent a business (although not a trade, unless significant additional services are provided), but the words 'as a going concern' indicate something more than purely passive income. The activity must involve some positive aspects to enable it to be transferred 'as a going concern', but this need not be restricted to the types of activities which are normally regarded as trades.

Creating a Cessation of the Business

Whichever method of transfer you choose, the income tax implications will be broadly the same. The business carried on by the individual will cease and a new business will be carried on by the company.

One of the effects of the transfer will be to create a cessation so that a 'drop out' can be calculated in the manner explained in Chapter 2. You have the opportunity to choose the date of transfer, and therefore your date of cessation, with great precision. However, it is essential for all these calculations to be done well in advance so that the best position can be obtained – and it cannot be done with hindsight.

The date of transfer of a business to a company is a question of fact, it is not something which can be dealt with in retrospect. If a transfer is to take place on 30 April in a particular year, it must actually happen on that day and all the necessary formalities must be completed then. It is not possible to decide some time during June or July that 30 April was the best time for the transfer to have taken place and to prepare all the documentation as if that had occurred. It is too late.

Backdating the paperwork to suggest that the transfer had taken place on an earlier occasion so as to secure a tax advantage is likely to be a crime (in fact it is likely to be a number of different crimes, from false accounting under S. 17 of the Theft Act 1968, obtaining a pecuniary advantage by deception under s. 15 of the Theft Act 1968, to uttering a false instrument under the Forgery and Counterfeiting Act 1981, to name just a few) and you should not think twice (or even once) about such action.

With proper planning the tax advantages can be achieved with the full agreement of the Inland Revenue and there is no reasonable excuse for doing otherwise.

Stock Valuation

A particular opportunity arises in connection with the stock valuation, because the value of the closing stock will naturally affect the profits for the final period. Normally the stock will be purchased by the company and the amount paid for the stock will therefore be deductible as an expense in computing the company's profits. In these circumstances the closing stock of the business will be taken as the amount at which it is transferred to the company, whatever its market value. This is extremely helpful because you are therefore able to adjust the profits for the final period to obtain the best tax position.

Sometimes you will want to sell the stock to the company at a low value to reduce the profits for the final period. This will not only have an effect on the final period of trading, but may also enter into the calculation for the penultimate year (depending upon the date of cessation) so as to reduce the amount of the profits chargeable for that year as well. Furthermore, where the trader is chargeable to tax at the higher rate of tax, a low closing stock value will reduce the profits chargeable at the higher rate. This will inevitably mean that the profits of the company will be increased, because when the stock is sold the profit made by the company will be correspondingly higher; however, unless the profits are extremely large, the increase in the company's profit will be chargeable at the small companies' rate of 25 per cent, thereby giving rise to a tax saving of 15 per cent compared with the tax which would otherwise be payable by the trader.

Alternatively, there may be reasons (for example, your dropout calculations may require a high profit or you may have losses elsewhere that you can use) why a high profit is desirable in the final period of trading. In these circumstances you would transfer the stock to the company at a high value so as to increase the profit. The high transfer value will leave the company with little profit when the stock is sold and this will reduce the tax in the company.

Work-in-Progress Valuation

Similar considerations apply to work in progress, but in this case a further opportunity arises. Where the value of the work in progress exceeds cost you can elect to have the excess excluded from the final accounts. This does not mean that it escapes tax completely because it will be chargeable to tax in the year of receipt as a 'post-cessation receipt'. In effect this enables both the profits for the final trading period and the profits of the company to be reduced; this might not save any income tax because the post-cessation receipts will still be taxed, but the trader will receive these receipts without any charge to national insurance contributions.

Capital Allowances

When a trade ceases on a transfer to a company, any capital allowances claimed on the fixtures and fittings, and plant and machinery, will be partly recovered by treating the assets as being sold at market value. To avoid this disadvantage you can elect to have the assets transferred to the company at their book value for tax purposes. What this means is that the allowances continue to be given in the same amounts, but against the company's profits, as if there had been no transfer.

However, there is another alternative which can sometimes be much better. You can choose the value at which the assets are to be transferred to the company (as you would value stock and work in progress, see above). A high transfer value will cause the final profits of the trade to be increased because some of the earlier allowances will be clawed back, whereas a low value will give an additional allowance in the final trading period. Usually it will be better to have a low transfer value, particularly if the final trading profits are chargeable at a high rate of tax, but the figure can be adjusted to give you the very best tax position.

Timing the Transfer

Whenever a transfer to a company is contemplated a question arises about the level of profits at which the transfer will be worth while. There is no easy answer, because the transfer will depend upon a large number of factors which will be different in each particular case. For example, it would depend upon the level of profits dropping out of assessment on the cessation and the level of income the individual will need to receive from the company. The availability of other reliefs, including the possibility of significantly improved pension benefits through a company pension scheme (as opposed to personal pension policies), will also be relevant and the national insurance implications and other costs must also be taken into account.

It would be wrong to conclude that just because a trader has started to pay higher rate tax he would be better off transferring the business to a company where only the small companies' rate would be payable. He must take into account the level of his personal income requirements because if he needs, say, £50,000 a year to live on and would therefore need a salary of this amount from the company, he could be considerably worse off on a year-by-year basis. The salary would bear the same tax that would have been payable had he received it as profits as a sole trader, but the tax would be payable under PAYE at a much earlier date; the cash-flow disadvantage could be significant. Furthermore, his national insurance contributions would be substantially higher because the company will have to pay the employers' contribution of 10.4 per cent of salary without limit. Add to this the costs of incorporation and the extra costs of auditing which would be required for the company's accounts and the exercise could end up being wholly unprofitable. In the longer term there are also inheritance tax implications and the much more onerous conditions required to qualify for capital gains tax retirement relief in respect of the shares.

Capital Gains Tax

One of the most valuable loopholes for avoiding capital gains tax can arise when a business is incorporated, but first I should explain how capital gains tax operates on incorporation.

Where the whole of the assets of a business are transferred to a company in exchange for shares, and the business is transferred as a going concern, any capital gains which would have arisen on the transfer of the assets are not charged to capital gains tax. The capital gains which would have arisen are deducted from the value of the shares acquired in exchange for the business, so that the tax is effectively deferred until the shares are sold. Because the gains are therefore rolled into the shares, and because the trader and the company are connected persons, the company is treated for capital gains tax purposes as if it had acquired the business assets at market value – although no tax arises.

For example:

Consider the position of a sole trader who carries on business from freehold premises which cost him £50,000, but which are now worth £350,000. He may have in mind that in due course he would like to sell up, but would prefer not to pay tax on the capital gain on the freehold property. What he can do is to transfer the business to a company in exchange for shares so that he rolls over his capital gain into shares. If the company then sells the property for £350,000, there is no tax liability at all.

What has happened is that the company is treated as having acquired the property for £350,000, so the company does not make a gain when it sells the property for the same price. The capital gain has not completely disappeared, it has been rolled into the shares, but that does not matter because the sole trader is not selling the shares, he is selling the property. Therefore, the whole of the sale proceeds of the property are received by the company, and tax on a gain of £300,000 is avoided. This possibility alone is a good enough reason always to start a business as a sole trader and later transfer it to a company if there is any chance that assets (such as a property or even goodwill) will later be sold at a capital gain.

The sale proceeds will, of course, be retained by the company, but that is not particularly disadvantageous and well worth the complete avoidance of capital gains tax which in the above example would be over £100,000. The company can invest the money in any way you choose and all the income can be paid out to the shareholders as and when required; if it is retained by the company the income will bear corporation tax at an advantageous rate. The company will simply be the investment vehicle of the individual which contains the bulk of his savings. Provided the shares are never sold, and there is no reason why they should be, the capital gains tax will simply never arise.

Naturally, with such a substantial avoidance opportunity, great care must be taken with the procedure, because the Inland Revenue will not be slow to invoke the *Ramsay* doctrine if they can see any reason to regard the whole arrangement as a preordained series of transactions. However, with careful planning you should always be able to avoid this possibility.

Inheritance Tax

The transfer of a business to a company will not of itself give rise to any particular inheritance tax advantage, because in most cases the value of the trader's estate will be unchanged. Instead of his estate comprising the value of the business, including all the business assets, his estate will contain the shares in the company which carries on the business. However, if the transferer's shareholding in the company is significantly less than 100 per cent of his previous interest in the business, the value of his estate may be diminished.

Business property relief

In some circumstances the incorporation of the business could make the inheritance tax position considerably worse by reducing or eliminating your entitlement to business property relief. This is a special relief given for inheritance tax, and it operates by reducing the value of property brought into charge to tax. If you have a business, or if you have more than 25 per cent of the shares in your family trading company, the relief is 50 per cent and may shortly increase to 100 per cent; if your shareholding is 25 per cent or less you will be entitled to only 30 per cent possibly rising to 50 per cent relief. The lower rate of relief is also available against any property you own and which is used for the purpose of the business, or for the business of a company under your control.

If a business is being carried on in partnership by three partners who share profits in the ratio 3:1:1, the incorporation of the business will have a serious effect on the availability of business property relief for the two junior partners. Their interest in the business during the subsistence of the partnership would benefit from business property relief at the higher rate, irrespective of the size of their interests. Similarly any business assets owned by them and used by the partnership business would qualify for relief at the lower rate.

However, if the business were to be incorporated and their shareholdings were in the same proportion as their previous interest in the partnership, the junior partners would have only a 20 per cent shareholding entitling them to only the lower rate of business relief on their shares. They would also lose all entitlement to business property relief on assets owned personally and which are thereafter provided for the use of the company; business relief in these circumstances applies only to a controlling shareholder. Furthermore, even the 30 per cent relief on the shares would not be available until the shares had been held for 2 years.

Planning

The incorporation of the business still provides an excellent opportunity for inheritance tax planning. It is much easier to separate the ownership of the shares of the company from the running of the business, and shares in the family company are one of the easiest assets to give away. The nature of a shareholding rarely gives the shareholder any rights to obtain for himself the assets of the company. Obviously, an outright gift of 75 per cent of the shares would be somewhat dangerous as the donee could then wind up the company, but this is not a gift which is ever likely to be contemplated, unless the donor has the utmost faith in the judgement and responsibility of the donee!

However, a gift of part of a parent's shareholding, possibly to an accumulation and maintenance trust for the children, would enable the parent to retain a high degree of influence over the voting power so that the business could be continued without interference. The shares would still benefit from business property relief, providing the shares were retained by the donee and if the company is a trading company the gift would qualify for holdover relief for capital gains tax, so no capital gains tax liability need arise on the disposal.

How to Benefit from the Small Companies' Rate

The rate of corporation tax paid by companies on their profits depends upon the size of those profits. If the profits for the year are less than £250,000, the rate of tax is 25 per cent, whereas if the profits are more than £1.25 million, the rate of tax is currently 33 per cent. For profits in between you may think there ought to be a sliding scale so that the rate of tax gradually increases from 25 to 33 per cent. Unfortunately, it does not work like that. There is a complicated formula, but what it means is that profits above £250,000 are effectively chargeable to tax at a rate of 35 per cent until you reach the upper limit. This is calculated simply like this:

Tax on	£250000 @ 25%	=	62500
Tax on	£1250000 @ 33%	=	412500
	£1000000		£250000

Accordingly the £1 million in the intermediate band costs tax of £350,000 which is a rate of 35 per cent. This has a number of implications, the most obvious being that any tax-deductible expense of a company with profits in this band will be worth 35 per cent in terms of tax relief, instead of only 25 per cent.

An obvious way of improving the benefit of the small companies' rate would be to have two companies each with profits of £250,000; however the Inland Revenue saw that one coming and where there are two or more companies under common control, the limit is divided between the number of companies. That sounds as if it might prevent exploitation of the rules, but fortunately it does not.

For example:

Two people who are not otherwise connected by family or other relationships are in business together, run a company in which they hold the shares half each; if the company makes £500,000 profits, the tax will be as follows:

£250000 @ 25%	=	62500
£250000 @ 35%	=	87500
£500000		£150000

However, if the company's business is capable of being divided into two parts, they could have two companies. One of the directors could have 51 per cent of the first company and 49 per cent of the second and the other director could have 49 per cent of the first company and 51 per cent of the second company. They would both be directors of both companies and continue to run them in exactly the same way; it is just that their shareholdings would be slightly different.

In this way the companies would not be under common control, because one director would control one company and the other director would control the other, and both companies would benefit from the full £250,000 small companies' rate; the tax would be reduced to £125,000. This need not interfere with the running of the business, but it would save £25,000 in tax.

However, there may be reasons why it is not possible to construct matters in this way. There may not be two persons running the business; there may be just one person controlling the business or perhaps a group of companies.

For example:
Say there is a group of three companies which consists of one main company which makes £240,000 profit and two little companies which make practically no profit at all. The small companies' limit of £250,000 will be divided between each of the companies, giving a small companies' rate limit of £83,333 chargeable at the 25 per cent rate. The tax paid by the main company would be computed as follows:

£ 83333 @ 25%	=	20833
£156667 @ 35%	=	54833
£240000		£75666

If the profits had been divided equally between the three companies so that they each made £80,000, each company would have been liable to tax at the small companies' rate of 25 per cent and the total tax would be £60,000. This manoeuvre would save £15,666.

Saving Tax in Employment

Expenses

In this book we are concerned with ways of saving tax which might not be immediately apparent, so I do not intend to dwell on the subject of obtaining a tax deduction for expenses against your income if you are employed and taxed under PAYE. Such expenses which may be allowed are very few and far between, and I only mention this subject to avoid a lot of wasted effort. To obtain a tax deduction from your earnings an expense must be incurred 'wholly, exclusively and necessarily' in the performance of the duties of the employment. The more you look at these words the worse they become and the test is interpreted by the Inland Revenue extremely strictly. It is not too cynical to say that the test simply cannot be satisfied. The expenses have to be *wholly and exclusively and necessarily incurred in the performance of the duties*. That means that you must incur the expense while performing your duties and you could not do the job without incurring it. The fact that it would enable you to do your job better is irrelevant. It may also be said with some justification that if the expenditure on something is so necessary, your employer ought to be duty-bound to supply it for you.

Even expenses which are absolutely essential to your job, such as the cost of travelling to and from your office, are not allowable because they are expenses incurred to put you in the position to perform your duties, not in the performance of the duties themselves. You may say that you need to buy a pen to write with, but again when you buy the pen you are merely putting yourself in a position to perform your duties. The act of buying pens is not part of your duties – unless, of course, your job is to conduct research into the attitude of retailers when selling new pens.

Practically every case that has come before the courts on this subject has failed. You may be lucky with a claim, but it is not very likely. However, it may be of passing interest to note that this extraordinarily strict provision, s. 198 of the Taxes Act 1988, allows a tax deduction for necessary expenses of travelling in the performance of the duties of the employment or of keeping and maintaining a *horse* to enable you to perform those duties. How this bizarre provision has survived is a mystery, and if you are obliged to travel by horse in the performance of your duties you have a clear right to a tax deduction for the costs of keeping and maintaining your horse. This, however, does not seem to be a fruitful source of tax advantage for most people.

Benefits in Kind

Everybody is familiar with benefits in kind. These are fringe benefits which go with a job and generally the more senior you are the more perks become available to you. The whole idea behind fringe benefits is that they are either tax free (which is not very likely) or they are taxed at a lower level than a straight salary. Therefore, your overall tax liability is reduced if you are provided with fringe benefits rather than having to pay for them yourself. In the last 20 years there has been an explosion in the provision of fringe benefits and the Inland Revenue have tried to discourage them by charging tax on benefits so that you end up paying the same tax anyway. However, there remain a number of benefits which are extremely valuable and should be on everybody's shopping list.

Note that some benefits are not taxable if you earn less than £8,500 per annum. The tax rules used to describe people earning more than £8,500 as 'higher paid', but inflation has rather overtaken this phrase; for some people, earnings of less than £8,500 would now be regarded as being below the official poverty line.

Company cars

Company cars are probably the most popular fringe benefit. In most cases you pay tax according to a scale based on the size of the car's engine, the age of the car and the original cost of the car when new. The scale is as follows for 1992/3:

	At End of Tax Year		
	Under 4 Yrs Old	Over 4 Yrs Old	Scale B
Cars costing up to £19,250:			
1400 cc or less	2140	1460	500
1401 cc to 2000 cc	2770	1880	630
Over 2000 cc	4440	2980	940
Cars costing £19,251 to £29,000	5750	3870	940
Cars costing over £29,000	9300	6170	940

This seems straightforward enough; you look at the characteristics of your car and read off your taxable benefit from the scale. However, there are lots of additional rules which enable you to gain an advantage.

Here are some tips on reducing the Scale Benefit.

- If you drive more than 18,000 miles each year on business the scale benefit is reduced by half; alternatively if you drive less than 2,500 miles on business the scale benefit is increased by half. It is blindingly obvious to say that if your mileage is in the middle you do not have a lot of scope, but if you are near either limit you should make quite sure that you drive a few more miles on business so as to take you over the relevant limit. If, for example, the end of the year is approaching and you have driven 16,000 miles on business and your scale benefit would normally be £5,500, driving an extra 2,000 miles deliberately on business will halve your scale charge and probably save you £1,100 in tax. This is clearly worth while and you should therefore keep a careful record of each journey so that you can demonstrate to the Inland Revenue that you are entitled to this 50 per cent reduction.

- The tax saving does not end there because if you are also subject to the car fuel benefit (see below) that will be halved as well. At the other end of the scale, if you hardly drive you car on business at all you can again save £1,100 by making sure that you drive more than 2,500 miles on business. Strangely, the car fuel benefit is not increased even if you drive less than 2,500 miles on business.

- If you have a car provided by your own company you will be equally interested in your company's liability to national insurance and VAT on the provision of the car. The company will be liable to national insurance contributions and VAT on the same scales, so that if you can reduce the scale charge on the main benefit everything else will go down in proportion.

- The company car benefit is charged if the car is 'available for your use' and it does not matter whether you actually use the car or not. However, there is a relaxation if the car is not available for a period of at least 30 consecutive days. So, if you are going on holiday or on a business trip for 3 weeks, you might like to invite your employer to take back the car for 30 days so that it is not available for your use. This may leave you without a car for a few days (depending upon when the weekends fall during your holiday), so that it is unavailable for 30 consecutive days. This will only save you about £200 in tax, depending upon the type of car, but it is a reasonable reward for a few days' inconvenience.

- If you are able to choose your car, it is obviously much more tax effective to choose a car just below the price or engine size threshold. For example, by choosing a 1.9 litre car costing under £19,251, rather than one just above these limits, you will reduce your scale charge by £2,850 and save over £1,100 tax each year.

- If your employer, as a condition of providing you with a car, requires you to make a financial contribution for having the car provided to you, the amount you pay will be deducted from the scale charge. This is not generally an advantage because for every £100 you pay in contribution, your tax will go down by £40, assuming you pay tax at the higher rate. This is not a good bargain and it should be avoided if possible. However, if you do make such a contribution you should ensure that you are *required* to pay it as a condition of having the car; otherwise the amount you pay will simply be ignored and your tax liability will be entirely unaffected.

- You should always make sure that all the costs of the car are paid for by the employer. You receive no reduction in your scale charge if, for example, you pay privately for the servicing.

- You may think that it would be a good idea not to have a car at all, but to have a van. There is some substance in this point because the scale benefit does not apply to vehicles which are not commonly used as private vehicles or are not suitable to be so used, such as lorries, vans (e.g. motor repair vans) or vehicles with a flashing light (e.g. a fireman's car). However, although this gets you out of the scale benefit, it will do you no good at all, because other provisions will apply instead and you could end up paying a lot more tax on this benefit under the general provisions.

Car fuel

If your employer pays for your private petrol you are taxed on that as well and the amounts you pay are shown in Scale B. It is obviously a matter of calculation whether it is better to pay for the fuel yourself or to have your employer pay for the fuel and for you to pay the tax on the benefit. But there are no half-measures; if the employer pays for any part of your fuel you pay the tax on the full scale benefit. You can reduce the scale charge by half if you drive more than 18,000 miles per annum on business and the same comments made above in connection with the main scale apply equally to the fuel scale – except that it does not apply to increase the fuel scale if you drive less than 2,500 miles.

If you are required by your employer to make a contribution towards the fuel it will only affect the amount of your taxable benefit if the whole of your private petrol is reimbursed. If you reimburse 99 per cent of the private petrol you will still be liable to the full fuel scale and be considerably worse off – you will effectively be paying twice.

If you drive a car which uses diesel fuel you should be aware that the rates of car fuel benefit are likely to be reduced before long to reflect the reduced cost of diesel.

Car parking

An exceptionally valuable fringe benefit is the provision of a car parking space, particularly in city centres where a car parking space can almost cost more than the car itself. For reasons which are probably more to do with the fact that government buildings have car parking spaces for their employees (including the Inland Revenue's head office in the Strand), the provision of a car parking space is not a taxable benefit. Nor will any taxable benefit arise if your employer pays for the parking space, or reimburses you for your parking costs.

Car telephones

If you have a telephone in your car (or a mobile phone which you can carry around) you will pay tax on a flat rate benefit of £200 per annum. You can claim that it is a valuable business tool and essential to your job, but you will still pay the tax unless you can show that there is no private use of the telephone at all, or that you reimburse your employer for the full cost of any private use. In some cases the best way out of any tax liability is to encourage your employer to apply for a 'dispensation' from the Inland Revenue.

A dispensation is an agreement reached with the Inland Revenue which says that the particular expenditure does not actually give rise to any taxable benefit on the employee and can therefore be ignored for tax purposes. This can apply to many types of expenditure. In the context of car phones, if the employer can persuade the Inland Revenue that the provision of a car telephone to its employee is strictly controlled, and all private calls are monitored and paid for by the employee, they will sometimes agree that no taxable benefit arises.

Living accommodation

If your employer provides you with living accommodation, that is another benefit in kind upon which you will pay tax. At the present time the tax is based on a notional rent equal to the gross rateable value; however since the abolition of the rates and the introduction of the community charge there are no rateable values, so the old rateable value will be used until a new system is devised. The point here is that rateable values tend to be rather low so this means that the benefit and therefore the tax will also be very low. A flat with a gross rateable value of £2,000 will therefore give rise to a tax charge of £800 per annum, which is not a bad price to pay for having a flat in a city centre!

Unfortunately, it is not quite as simple as that because if the living accommodation costs more than £75,000, you will be charged a supplementary benefit on a percentage (presently about 11 per cent) on the excess over £75,000 and this can make the tax charge on the living accommodation extremely expensive. For example, if your employer buys a flat in London for £175,000, you will not only pay tax on the rateable value but also on the supplement of £11,000 (being £100,000 at 11 per cent); the total tax might be as much as £100 per week. In addition, if there is any furniture provided in the flat you will be charged an extra benefit for the use of the furniture and other assets in the flat, and the tax liability on the total benefits begins to get out of control. With property prices as they are in city centres, a convenient flat is unlikely to be available for less than £75,000, so a means has to be found of avoiding this supplementary charge.

You might, for example, purchase the flat jointly with your employer so that his proportion does not cost more than £75,000. This would give rise to a benefit based only on the rateable value and no supplementary charge would arise. This would be a good deal cheaper than having an interest-free loan from your employer of £75,000, but of course you would lose the capital appreciation (and possibly the capital gains tax private residence exemption) on that part of the flat which belongs to the employer and this is clearly something to be taken into account.

Buying the property jointly with your employer also enables you to claim that there should be no benefit at all because of a loophole. The rules which charge tax on this benefit say that you only pay tax if the living accommodation is provided by reason of your employment. You can argue with some force that your employer does not provide it for you. Because you are a joint owner you are entitled, by virtue of your own interest in the property, to occupy the property as of right. You do not need your joint owner's permission, nor can he claim any rent from you.

However, it is unlikely to be a good idea for your employer to provide you with your main residence. You can obtain exemption from capital gains tax on your main residence and the loss of the opportunity to make a substantial tax-free capital gain should not lightly be disregarded.

It may be that you do not have the funds available to purchase the house of your choice. The best of all worlds would be for your employer to purchase the residence and to grant you an option to buy the house at some time in the future at today's price. In that way you have the house provided for you without having to pay for it (although you would pay tax on the benefit of having the house provided for you), but in due course when you have the funds available you can exercise your option and purchase the house at the original price. You will later be able to obtain the large capital when you sell the house entirely free of tax, because it is exempt through being your main residence. The option is unlikely to be particularly valuable because, at the date the option is granted, the value of the benefit is pretty small. What is the value of the right to buy a house presently worth £200,000 for £200,000? Not a great deal. What is valuable is the opportunity to purchase the house at this price at some time in the future and this should be taken into account in determining the value of the option when granted.

In any event, the taxable benefit of having an option granted in this way is likely to be small and the tax liability on the benefit of the option will be even smaller – particularly in comparison with the ultimate gain you intend to make.

Here is a word of warning, however. If you exercise the option to buy immediately before you intend to sell the house, you will find that the Inland Revenue will refuse to allow the private residence exemption for capital gains tax. It is essential that you exercise the option and live in the house for a reasonable period so that it cannot justifiably be said by the Inland Revenue that you acquired the house wholly or partly for the purposes of realising a gain from its disposal.

There is another means of exploiting the precise wording of the legislation to provide a property for your private use. The employer could lend you some money interest free with which you would then be able to buy the property of your choice. Unfortunately, a simple loan will not work at all because you will be taxed heavily on the benefit of having an interest-free loan. The Inland Revenue apply a special rate of interest (known as the 'official rate'), which is the same as that used for calculating the benefit on property costing over £75,000. The result is that you could be worse off.

However, you could establish a trust for your own benefit, and your employer could make an interest-free loan to the trust of the money you require. Because of a loophole in the legislation a loan to a trust does not give rise to a benefit. The trustees could then, if they wanted, buy the property which you have in mind. Provided the money was lent unconditionally, it could not justifiably be said that the property was provided by reason of your employment. It would be provided at the discretion of the trustees and would have nothing to do with your employment. The benefit provided by the employer is the interest-free loan, but because of the defect in the rules, that benefit does not give rise to a tax charge.

The loophole is rather limited in its scope because if the employer is a company and you are a director of the company, such a loan might be unlawful under the Companies Act and could not therefore be made. If you are a shareholder in a private company it is possible that the Inland Revenue would argue that the loan could be treated as a 'loan to a participator', giving rise to the need to deposit with the Inland Revenue an additional amount equal to one-third of the loan, until the loan is repaid. However, there is a very strong argument that these provisions do not apply to loans to trustees; the rules relate only to loans to individuals – and trustees are not individuals. But for senior employees of large companies this can be a very attractive strategem.

Avoid the benefit by getting a cash alternative

There is a general principle which applies to the taxation of fringe benefits which is that if the benefit is convertible into money the above rules will not always apply. If you have a cash option it is the cash convertibility value which is the measure of the benefit.

If your employer says that you can have a company car or you can have an increase in salary of £5,000 and you can surrender the car at any time and receive the higher salary, the measure of the benefit to you is £5,000; that is the amount upon which you will be taxed – not the scale benefit. If the scale charge would have been only £2,500 you are clearly losing out, so you would be very wise to avoid such an arrangement. Unfortunately, with cars it does not work the other way round; if the cash option was only £1,000, you would *still* be taxed on the higher scale charge. The charging provisions for company cars say that where a car is provided for you by reason of your employment and the benefit is not otherwise chargeable to tax as your income, you pay tax on the figures according to the scale. The benefit is that found from the scale, so if you are not taxed on the full scale benefit you do not escape the charge.

However, the rules for taxing the various different benefits are not all the same and the differences in wording can make this an effective technique for other benefits such as the provision of living accommodation.

In the case of living accommodation, the rules say that you will be taxed on the benefit, unless the living accommodation is 'otherwise made the subject of any charge' on you by way of income tax. So, if you are provided with a flat which would normally give rise to a benefit of £10,000 per annum under the benefits legislation, but you are able to surrender your right to occupy the flat and have a £500 pay rise instead, you will be taxable only on the £500 and not the £10,000. This is because the living accommodation would be made the subject of a charge to income tax on you, that is £500, and accordingly the charging provisions for the benefit of living accommodation would not apply.

Golden Handshakes

The term 'golden handshake' is an emotive one describing payments made on the termination of a person's employment. It derives from an earlier era when there was a distinction in tax treatment between compensation for loss of office and *ex gratia* payments. Compensation for loss of office is exactly what it says; it is compensation, more accurately described as damages for breach of contract. If the employer breaches the employment contract by terminating it prematurely, like anybody else who does not meet his contractual obligations, he must pay damages.

However, an *ex gratia* payment is entirely different. It is a payment for which there is no obligation and it is made freely by the employer for his own reasons when somebody has left his employment, usually after a long period of loyal service. The tax treatment of these amounts is now the same and it may be more convenient to describe them both as lump sums.

The important point about a lump sum as far as the recipient is concerned is that it can be tax free up to £30,000. If the lump sum is greater than £30,000 the excess is taxed as earnings in the normal way. It is therefore crucial that you make sure that, if you are ever likely to be in a position of receiving such a lump sum, you get the first £30,000 tax free. It is obviously very expensive in terms of tax if you don't take this opportunity. The basic rule is that if you receive payment as a reward for your services it will be taxable.

For example, if your contract of employment provides that you will receive compensation of one year's salary if the contract is terminated for any reason, the first £30,000 exemption will not be available. The reason for this is that your contract of employment provides for you to work on certain terms. These terms will include your salary, your holiday entitlement and various other benefits, including the right to the lump sum on termination. It is therefore part of the terms on which you are working and is thus part of the reward for your services. What you need to do is to avoid any such terms or even understandings to this effect, so that if your contract is broken you receive damages for breach of contract and not the fulfilment of the terms of the contract. In this way the first £30,000 will be tax free, instead of it being taxed in full as earnings.

There is another opportunity to obtain the tax-free lump sum of £30,000, which is if the payment is made in connection with the termination of the employment by reason of death, or on account of injury or disability. This means that if an employee is injured or becomes disabled, he or his dependants would be eligible to the £30,000 exemption in respect of any payments made by the employer for this reason. This is not really a loophole because it is not a matter within the power of the employee to obtain such a payment, but it can be useful to draw the employer's attention to the possibility. He may feel much more generously inclined to his former employee or his dependants if he can provide them with a substantial tax advantage, perhaps by making a lump sum payment instead of a pension, which would be taxable in full when it is received.

Unapproved retirement benefits schemes?

There has been a recent change in the approach of the Inland Revenue to the subject of *ex gratia* payments. They have taken the view that such payments (other than genuine redundancy payments) are really unapproved retirement benefits schemes and are thus taxable in full. This is a highly controversial view but, as always, it is better to avoid difficulties wherever possible and such payments should therefore never be made pursuant to any agreement or arrangement with the employer. Indeed, the employer would be doing his employee a favour if he did not disclose the possibility at all before payment. Having regard to the sensitivity of these payments it would be wise to take professional advice whenever such a payment is contemplated.

Termination payments for the self-employed

Although such lump sums are most commonly made in connection with the termination of an employment, they can also arise in connection with the termination of a professional relationship. If you are in business and a long-standing customer or client decides to go elsewhere you might receive a lump-sum payment by way of testimonial. Such a payment, providing it is entirely voluntary and not made as a reward for past services, but merely as a solatium for the termination of the relationship, will not be a taxable receipt.

Single Premium Bonds

A reasonably common investment is a single premium bond, which is really a non-qualifying insurance policy, on the joint lives of the policyholder and his spouse. On the death of the spouse the benefits under policy arise and an income tax charge arises.

If the bond is held in trust the charge would still arise on the settlor of the trust. If the policyholder arranges for his will to provide that on his death the bond is held in trust for his wife, on her death the charge would not arise on her (which it would do if she had been the beneficial owner), but on the husband because he established the trust. However, he would no longer be alive and not a taxpayer, so no charge to income tax would arise.

More Ways of Saving Tax for Proprietors

Additional Relief for Interest Paid on Loans

Many proprietors of businesses have to provide their own capital to help fund the business. The business may well be financed partly by a bank loan or a bank overdraft, but invariably the proprietor will have to provide money as well. He may borrow money personally and inject that money into the business, but usually his contribution to the funding is to restrict the amount of profit he draws out. The situation will be familiar; the business makes £50,000 profit, but because of the state of the cash flow, the proprietor only draws out £2,000 per month. This means that he will leave undrawn profits in the business of

£26,000 for the year and this will swell his proprietor's capital amount. Over the years the balance on his capital account can become substantial.

For example:
A trader wishes to move house and he needs a mortgage of £80,000 to assist with the purchase. He knows that tax relief will only be available on the interest on the first £30,000 of borrowings and he resigns himself to forgoing tax relief on the extra £50,000. He might like to draw some money out of the business, but if the bank account is on or near the overdraft limit, that might not be possible.

However, what he can do is withdraw £50,000 from the business bank account for the house purchase, thereby reducing his mortgage to the £30,000 limit, and subsequently borrow £50,000 to restore the business bank account to its previous level. The reason why this is so advantageous is that borrowing money to lend to your business is a qualifying purpose as far as interest is concerned and all the interest will be tax deductible. In this way tax relief is obtained on the whole of the £80,000. And what is more, although interest on the first £30,000 will qualify for relief at the basic rate only, interest on the £50,000 balance will be eligible for relief at the higher rate.

The order in which you do this is of the utmost significance, because if you borrow money and lend it to your business, the interest relief stops if you later recover the money from the business. So if you put the money in first and then withdraw it, you will receive no relief. If you withdraw the money first and then replace it, the provisions regarding recovery of capital will not apply.

It is essential that the money borrowed to put in the business is used wholly for the purposes of the trade; however this should not be in any serious doubt. Indeed, having drawn rather a lot of money out, the business is in rather greater need than it was before and it should be comparatively simple to show that the money was used wholly for business purposes.

One difficulty with the above arrangements is a technical provision which states that if a scheme has been effected or arrangements have been made, the sole or main benefit of which is that a tax deduction is obtained for interest payments, the relief can be denied. It is unusual for the Inland Revenue to invoke this provision in connection with this arrangement, but in case they are tempted to do so, you should ensure that the borrowings fulfil other commercial purposes as well – such as a variation of the security for the borrowings.

A better way would be to avoid the problem altogether by simply allowing the business bank overdraft to be increased. Your overall borrowings would be the same, but the configuration would be different and, although the overdraft may give rise to a higher rate of interest, this would be more than compensated by the tax relief which would be available.

Industrial Buildings Allowances

An industrial building is a building which is used for the purpose of a qualifying trade. A qualifying trade is the manufacture or process of goods and materials, and buildings used to store goods for this purpose can also qualify. An industrial buildings allowance is available for the cost of construction of the building, but since 1986 the allowance is miserably low – only 4 per cent per annum. It is worth claiming because the costs of constructing a building are usually high, but it still takes 25 years to obtain the full allowance. There is not a lot of scope for tax saving here.

However, the allowances have not always been so low. Before 1986 the allowance was front-end loaded; an allowance of up to 75 per cent was given in the year the costs were incurred, and a further 4 per cent given in that year and in every subsequent year until the expenditure was fully relieved. This initial allowance was reduced in 1984 to 50 per cent and reduced again to 25 per cent in 1985, and thereafter no initial allowance was given. Industrial buildings allowances in enterprise zones are specially treated and qualify for 100 per cent allowance in the year the expenditure is incurred.

Enterprise zones are particular areas of the country designated by the government where business activity is encouraged by various tax and other privileges. These include improved customs facilities, favourable treatment regarding the uniform business rate and enhanced capital allowances, including industrial buildings allowances on expenditure which would not otherwise qualify for any tax relief.

The allowances are given until tax relief has been given for all the expenditure, but if you sell your interest in the building within 25 years the allowances are clawed back and you pay tax on a balancing charge equal to the allowances withdrawn.

For example:

Costs of construction in 1984		500000
Initial allowance 50%	250000	
Writing down allowance 1984–91		
7 years @ 4%	140000	
	———	390000
Residue not yet allowed		£110000

You can carry on claiming the 4 per cent per annum until 1997, but let us assume you wish to sell the property in 1992 for £600,000. You would not pay capital gains tax on this because indexation relief will apply to absorb all the gain, but you would still have to pay tax on the £390,000, being the allowances clawed back. It may be said that you are no worse off because you are only giving back the tax relief which you have previously claimed in earlier years. However, it would obviously be much better if you could sell the property and not have to pay tax on the allowances – and better still if you could sell the property, avoid the tax and continue to obtain the 4 per cent allowance each year. A careful reading of the legislation enables this to be achieved.

When expenditure is incurred the person who incurs the expenditure is entitled to the industrial buildings allowance. The interest he has in the building at that time is known as the relevant interest. If that relevant interest is disposed of the allowances are clawed back. So, to avoid a clawback of the allowance, you have to dispose of the building without disposing of the relevant interest.

If, for example, you have a freehold building, the grant of a lease, even a 999-year lease which is effectively the same as selling the freehold, will not give rise to the disposal of the relevant interest, because the relevant interest is the freehold; no matter how long a lease you grant, you will retain the freehold.

The same applies if you have a leasehold interest. If you assign your lease you would dispose of your relevant interest, but if you grant a sublease for the length of your own lease less a few days, you will keep the relevant interest. In this way you can effectively sell the building completely, but you will not have to give up the allowances you have previously claimed.

To make it even better, if the person who requires the building carries on a qualifying trade (which must be rather likely because why else would he want to buy the building?), you will continue to be entitled to the 4 per cent allowance each year, until the full expenditure is relieved.

Working Abroad

If you are going to work abroad you have some valuable opportunities to save some tax, but the rules vary depending on whether you are employed or self-employed.

Becoming Non-Resident

If you are abroad for long enough (or you get your timing right) so that you lose your UK residence, you will not be taxed for the year in which you are not resident. However, if you are self-employed you are taxed on the preceding year basis. You do not cease to trade just because you go abroad, as your profits will continue to be calculated and taxed in the same way. If you are non-resident for just 1 year, it will not be your earnings while you are away which escape tax; they will be taxed in the following year, when you have returned to the UK. The profits escaping tax will be those for the year which forms the basis period for your year of non-residence which will be the year before you go abroad.

For example, if you make up your accounts for the year ended 30 April 1992, those profits will be taxed in 1993/4. If you are non-resident for the whole of 1993/4 (which at the very least means that you must be outside the UK from 6 April 1993 to 5 April 1994 – see further Chapter 1), those profits will not be taxed. This long time-lag means that you have lots of time to plan your foreign engagements. So if your year ended 30 April 1992 was a really bumper year, you have nearly a year to make arrangements to be working abroad for 1993/4 so that you can be non-resident in that year and avoid tax on the whole of the 1992 profits. You would not have to leave the country until 5 April 1993.

Remaining UK Resident

However, you may not be able to be away for long enough to take advantage of this 1-year drop out; alternatively you may not want to be away for the whole tax year, as it may not do your business or your family any good. Indeed, if the reason why you are going to work abroad is to earn lots of money, this plan will be quite hopeless for avoiding tax on that income because those big profits will be taxed on the preceding year basis when you come back.

In these cases you should consider the 100 per cent deduction. This is a special relief which applies if you are employed abroad and can effectively provide exemption from tax on your earnings. There is no need to be non-resident, indeed it is essential that you remain UK resident, but you do have to plan your trips away with great care. The rules are rather complicated, but once they are grasped they can be used to great advantage.

The first thing you must do is to establish what is known as a qualifying period of absence of at least 365 days. This does not mean that you have to be away for 365 days, because you can make as many visits as you like to the UK, provided the days spent in the UK are in the right configuration. To satisfy the requirements for a qualifying period of absence, you have to look at each of the periods that you spend abroad and compare it with the periods that you spend in the UK. Each period of absence from the UK, however short, is known as a 'relevant period'. The combination of two relevant periods together with the intervening days spent in the UK is known as a 'qualifying period', provided that the intervening days in the UK are not more than 62 consecutive days, nor more than one-sixth of the total period. Each successive qualifying period creates a cumulative period and once the total cumulative period exceeds 365 days you get the 100 per cent deduction.

To simplify this, here is an example.

A	B	C	D	E	F	G	H
25	7	40	26	101	33	165	
	HOME		HOME		HOME		

Looking at the above example A–B and C–D are relevant periods because they are days of absence, and B–C are intervening days in the UK. The total period A–D is 72 days. The 7 intervening days are less than one-sixth of the total period so A–D is a qualifying period.

You now move on to the larger period, A–F, and do the same calculations. This is a total period of 199 days. There are two periods of UK presence totalling 33 days which is less than one-sixth of the total period, so A–F is a qualifying period as well.

Moving on to the third period, A–H, this is a total period of 397 days. The intervening periods in the UK total 66 days, which is less than one-sixth of the total period and there is no UK period of more than 62 consecutive days. So now we have a qualifying period of 365 days or more and the earnings for the period will qualify for the 100% deduction, i.e. they are effectively exempt from tax.

It is necessary to go through this complicated procedure to understand what you can do with the rules. You will see that it is not only the days in the UK which are important, but the days abroad immediately following a UK visit. So you can always do your calculations to make sure that you do not breach the one-sixth rule. You should always leave some flexibility in case you miss a flight or have to return home unexpectedly for a business or domestic crisis.

There is nothing in the rules which says that the days of absence from the UK have to be spent working; a holiday outside the UK is just as much a period of absence as a business trip. Nor do you have to be in the same job. You can come home each time and go away on a new assignment or, indeed, just go off looking for a new job. But you must be employed. The deduction is not available to self-employed individuals, however, so you must ensure that the nature of your work and the contract under which you are working is a contract of employment satisfying all the relevant tests for employment explained in Chapter 2. That is not likely to cause difficulty, because it will usually coincide with your employer's wishes.

If you are unable to satisfy the 365 days because you are not working abroad for long enough, all is not lost. As I explained above, the days abroad do not have to be spent working and you can still save the tax on the foreign earnings if you continue to make foreign trips just for shopping, holiday, visiting relatives or anything; you just have to be away. So if your employment is a little short, you can supplement it with holidays at the end and ensure that the earnings you do make benefit from the 100 per cent deduction.

A couple of months off in France, working on your holiday home, could be extremely valuable in terms of tax saving. The opportunity to do this seems entirely unintended, because there used to be a provision that the days abroad had to be substantially devoted to the duties of the employment, but this requirement was repealed with some earlier legislation and nothing replaced it for the purposes of the 100 per cent deduction.

In doing all these calculations you should always remember that the 100 per cent deduction applies only to individuals who are both resident and ordinarily resident in the UK. The earnings must be attributable to a qualifying period throughout which the individual was UK resident. Furthermore, you cannot count as a period of absence any days spent outside the UK during which you were resident abroad. So, if you come back to the UK after a period of non-residence, you cannot take that period into account at all in calculating your qualifying period.

Foreign Domiciled Individuals

If you are not domiciled in the UK, your position is much more advantageous. You are then able to benefit from the 'remittance basis' rules, which means that you only pay tax on your earnings if you bring them here.

To gain this extraordinary advantage your duties need to be performed wholly abroad and you must be employed by a non-resident employer. However, there is no 365-day period required, or anything like it, and it matters little how long you are away. You must make sure that your duties are performed wholly abroad and not partly in the UK; if you have to work in the UK you should have a separate contract for your foreign duties to protect those earnings from UK tax. It is highly likely that you would be working for a non-resident employer, but it is important to make sure that this is the case. Then your earnings from the employment will be entirely tax free, unless you bring them to the UK, which in most cases will be entirely unnecessary.

National Insurance Contributions

The trouble with national insurance contributions (NIC) is that they do not usually amount to very much money and further-more you know that there is actually some benefit to be derived from paying them – a full contribution record entitles you to all the wide range of social security benefits such as unemployment benefit, maternity pay and hundreds more. But there is no point in paying more contributions than you need. There is a max-imum level of contributions of £1,931 for 1992/3, payable by each individual, and if you pay more than the maximum it is a complete waste – you do not become entitled to any greater benefits.

If you have a single employment it is most unlikely that you will pay more than you should – the PAYE and NIC deduction rules mean that the proper amount is usually deducted from your salary each month. But if you have more than one job (or if you are employed and have self-employed business as well), you can end up paying too much. The DSS will not repay any excess to you – you will have to claim it back – so it is well worth keeping a record of the contributions you pay so that you can claim a refund if necessary.

The Labour Party have announced their firm intention to abolish the upper limit for employees' NIC so that employees would pay contributions on the whole of their earnings – just like employers. The points discussed on the next page for saving employers' contributions would be equally effective in saving employees' contributions should this change take place.

Employer's Contribution

However, if you are in business and employing staff you will not only be concerned with your own contributions; you will be just as concerned in the contributions you have to pay on behalf of your employees. This is called the employer's contribution and it can be enormous. An employer has to pay contributions of 10.4 per cent of the salary of his employees and there is no maximum, so if you are employing five people at £20,000 per annum you will have to pay out £10,400 in NIC. It would be a very good idea to arrange matters so that these contributions are reduced.

Benefits in Kind

One technique, which unfortunately is no longer available, was to pay your employees a bonus by giving them unit trusts. Although this loophole was stopped in November 1991, it is worth explaining how it worked because the same principles can apply in different ways.

The idea was that if you wanted to pay a bonus of (say) £50,000 to your employees, you bought £50,000 of unit trusts. Having done so you then decided to give the units to your staff as a reward for their services. You had to be careful not to provide any cash alternative and to ensure that the units were yours to give away before any entitlement to bonus arose. Having transferred the unit trusts to the employees, they could sell them and receive the money, and there would be no NIC payable by you or your employees.

This did not save any income tax because the value of the unit trusts was always earnings for tax purposes, although PAYE did not apply and the employee obtained a significant cash-flow advantage by not having to pay the tax for a year or so. However, they were not earnings for national insurance contributions purposes and you saved the employer's contributions of 10.4 per cent on the amount of bonuses. Although this no longer works for unit trusts or any other financial instrument, it can still work for other things such as goods which a particular employee may want.

For example:
An employee of yours is moving house and you become aware that he may like some new hi-fi equipment, various white goods or perhaps a new kitchen. It is quite possible for the company to buy the relevant assets itself and subsequently to transfer these goods to the employee by way of a bonus. There must be no cash alternative, nor must there be any prior entitlement to the bonus. However it is quite within the power of the employer to make some enquiries and buy some goods in the hope and expectation that they will be welcomed by the employee. This would save 10.4 per cent employer's contribution on the value of the goods supplied.

Dividends

It is not quite so easy for directors of family companies to follow this bonus route in respect of their own earnings, because the chances of persuading the DSS that it is not all prearranged may be extremely difficult if you are the person making the decision. What you need is a means by which you can receive money from the company, without the company having to incur the substantial extra cost of national insurance contributions. A dividend on the shares is a good solution, because dividends are not subject to national insurance contributions; neither are they subject to PAYE, so you obtain a cash-flow advantage as well.

Dividends are not tax deductible, but provided the company is profitable, the effect is the same. When a company pays a dividend it must pay advance corporation tax over to the Inland Revenue of an amount equal to one-third of the dividend. The recipient is treated as receiving the dividend net of basic rate tax and only has to pay the additional 15 per cent on the gross equivalent to bring his liability up to 40 per cent if he is liable to the higher rate of tax – but that extra tax is not payable until 1

December following the year in which the dividend was paid. The company has to pay advance corporation tax soon after dividend is paid, but this tax is recovered against its corporation tax liability for the period in which the dividend is paid.

For example:
If your company makes up its accounts to 30 April each year and you pay a dividend on 6 April 1992 of £15,000, the company has to pay over advance corporation tax of £5,000 on 14 May 1992. This £5,000 will be deductible from its corporation tax liability for the year ended 30 April 1992, leaving the company no worse off, except for the short timing difference. You receive the £15,000, which is treated as gross income of £20,000 from which £5,000 has been deducted, i.e. the basic rate of 25 per cent. If you are liable to tax at the higher rate you will have to pay an extra £3,000 on 1 December 1993.

Temporary Work in the UK

If a person normally works abroad and is not ordinarily resident in this country, but is sent here to work, he will be entitled to a 52-week period of grace during which he will not be liable to national insurance contributions. This applies both to the employee's contributions and to the employer's contributions, so both will have a keen interest in the arrangements.

That is all very well for the first 52 weeks, but you can gain an extra 52 weeks by arranging for the employee to work abroad for a short period immediately before the 52-week period expires; when he comes back the 52-week period will start all over again. You cannot keep doing this because the employee will soon become ordinarily resident in the UK, but it will work as long as he remains not ordinarily resident. (However, this will not be effective if he comes from a country where there is a national insurance reciprocal arrangement in force.)

Working Abroad

In the converse case a UK employee who goes to work abroad in a place where there is no reciprocal national insurance agreement will remain liable to national insurance contributions (and so will the employer) for 52 weeks following his departure. To avoid this 52-week period of continuing liability, you should arrange for the overseas employment not to commence until after the employee has ceased to be resident in the UK. In that case he will not satisfy the crucial test of being resident here immediately before commencing the foreign employment and the 52-week period will not apply.

There is no reason why the two employments cannot be with the same employer, but if so care should be taken to ensure that the foreign employment is not merely a variation of the first contract of employment.

Other Ideas

At the time of writing there are a number of other techniques being actively pursued by employers to avoid NIC – and which would be equally effective in avoiding the employees' contributions. One popular scheme involves vouchers whereby an employee receives his bonus in vouchers exchangeable at high street retailers, supermarkets and travel companies. These are fine for modest bonuses, but where the bonus is very large, they may not be entirely appropriate – after all who would want £250,000 worth of Sainsbury vouchers!

Another scheme involves the payment of the bonus in gold bars which can be sold fairly quickly for cash. However, it is highly complex and cannot sensibly be entertained without professional advice. Furthermore it is possible that the idea may no longer be available at the date of publication because the law can change very quickly to stop these schemes – although without affecting arrangements which have already been made. Even if this were to occur, some variation on the same theme will be devised and you should check the current position with a professional adviser.

=4=

HOW TO USE TRUSTS

What is a Trust?

Trusts are very important in connection with tax saving. They are the product of centuries of ingenuity by English lawyers and, although they are useful vehicles for tax planning, they can also play a valuable and essential role in the preservation of wealth for a family or any class of persons.

Trusts can be extremely useful as a means of ensuring that the family's wealth remains in responsible hands, and does not pass into the control of others who may be too young, too old or otherwise unable to deal with the property satisfactorily, particularly when large sums are involved. Traditionally this was helpful in the case of young daughters to protect their inheritance from the grasp of unworthy suitors! But a trust is equally appropriate as a protection from improvident or financially unsophisticated beneficiaries. In modern times, this principle has been extended to enable a family business to remain under the control of experienced trustees, so that effective succession by the next generation can be secured at the appropriate time without the assets being lost or unnecessarily lost or dissipated by the ravages of taxation.

Trusts are always complex, usually being contained in a long trust deed and in language which can often be difficult to understand. However, they need not be contained in a formal document; trusts can be created orally or even by conduct, but if you need a trust to achieve a tax-saving purpose, professional advice will be essential.

Knowing something about trusts and how they work will help you to put forward some of the ideas elsewhere in this book. Let me explain briefly how trusts operate.

A trust is an arrangement whereby one person (the settlor) transfers property to another (the trustee) to hold for the benefit of others (the beneficiaries). The rights and obligations of these parties are entirely different and should not be confused.

The Settlor

The settlor is the person who establishes the trust or anybody else who transfers property to the trust. There can be more than one settlor of the same trust. The trust deed will specify the duties and obligations of the trustees, but once the settlement has been established the settlor will have no further power over the trustees or the property in the trust, except as provided by the trust deed. However, the settlor can retain a degree of influence by requiring the trustees to obtain his consent before doing certain things, and he can also reserve for himself the power to appoint new trustees. It must always be appreciated that the trustees will have the legal ownership of all the trust assets, so they should be chosen with great care.

The Trustees

The trustees actually own the assets of the trust, which are known as the 'settled property'. They do not hold them for their own benefit, but for the benefit of the persons named in the trust as beneficiaries.

The trustees must deal with the settled property in the manner set out in the trust deed, and they also have numerous obligations imposed upon them by law. Neither the settlor nor the beneficiaries can tell the trustees what to do, although the trustees must, at all times, act in the best interests of the beneficiaries. If the beneficiaries feel that the trust is being improperly administered or the settled property is being dealt with wrongly, they can seek a court order to put matters right.

In most cases, there will be two trustees and there is no reason why the settlor cannot be a trustee, although sometimes this will not be desirable for tax and other reasons.

The Beneficiaries

The beneficiaries are the persons named in the trust deed as the persons for whose benefit the trustees hold the settled property. The beneficiaries can be specific individuals or a class of persons (e.g. all the present and future children of the settlor), and the trust can make provision for adding or removing beneficiaries from the class. Only those beneficiaries within the beneficial class are capable of benefiting from the settled property and nobody else is entitled to do so. The settlor can be a beneficiary and this will often be desirable in order to secure tax advantages.

There are some very complicated rules about how long a trust can last and how long income arising from the settled property can be accumulated before being paid out to the beneficiaries. It is usual for the trust to last for 80 years, which is sufficient for most purposes.

The document establishing the settlement must be very carefully drawn up, because if there is any uncertainty about the terms of the settlement, or if the trust could last for longer than the permitted period, it may be void and fail totally to achieve any of its intended purposes.

Types of Trust

Bare Trust

This is not really a trust at all, despite having all the outward appearance of a trust. In fact, the trustees act as nominees, merely holding assets for another person absolutely. The assets belong absolutely to the beneficiary, who can call for them at any time, and may direct the trustee to act in accordance with his wishes as far as the property is concerned. Where the beneficiaries are infants, a bare trust will often give rise to a real trust imposed by the Trustee Act 1925.

This type of trust can give rise to a particular advantage for parents who would like to build up a fund for the benefit of their children during their minority. It is possible for such a fund to be generated tax free by the use of the children's personal allowances without the annual income being taxed as the parents' income. This aspect is explained in more detail in Chapter 5.

Fixed Interest Trust

A fixed interest trust is one where a beneficiary has a right to all or part of the income of the trust as it arises, without necessarily any entitlement to capital. The beneficiary may only have a right to the income for a limited period and it is possible for the trust deed to provide for the right to be revoked, e.g. if the beneficiary proves unworthy of benefit in the opinion of the settlor or the trustees. The beneficiary with a fixed interest is said to have an interest in possession, which is an extremely important concept for inheritance tax purposes, as we shall see.

The income of a fixed interest trust is charged to tax at the basic rate in the hands of the trustees and the net amount is paid to the beneficiary. If the beneficiary is liable to tax at the higher rate on his income, he will have a further tax liability to pay on his trust income. If he is not liable to tax he can claim a repayment of the tax paid by the trustees.

Discretionary Trust

A discretionary trust is a trust where the trustees have a discretion to decide which, if any, of the beneficiaries should receive money from a trust in the form of income or capital. This discretion can be extremely wide, although the trustees can be guided in the exercise of their discretion by the wishes of the settlor, if necessary.

The income of a discretionary trust is taxed at 35 per cent in the hands of the trustees and if any of the income is paid to a beneficiary, the beneficiary will be treated as having received the income after deduction of tax at 35 per cent. If the beneficiary is liable to tax at the higher rate, he will be assessed to this extra tax directly by the Inland Revenue. If he is not liable to tax at this rate, the beneficiary can claim a tax repayment. In certain circumstances, e.g. where the settlor or his spouse can obtain any kind of benefit from the trust, the trustees will not be chargeable to tax at all, but the income will be deemed, for tax purposes, to be the income of the settlor.

Accumulation and Maintenance Trust

An accumulation and maintenance trust is a type of discretionary trust for the benefit of infants and young people up to the age of 25. Such a trust attracts particularly favourable treatment for inheritance tax purposes. Usually, the trustees will pay income tax at 35 per cent on the income of the trust, but only until the infants reach the age of 18. However, it is important to note that if any income is paid to or for the benefit of a beneficiary who is unmarried and under the age of 18 from a trust set up by his parents, that income will be treated as the income of the parents for all tax purposes.

Exploiting Trusts to Save Tax

The income tax treatment of the various types of trusts has been mentioned briefly above, from which it may be appreciated that the Inland Revenue are able to prevent many of the obvious means of exploitation of trusts for income tax purposes. However, a number of opportunities remain.

- If the beneficiaries *are not* the children of the settlor, it is possible to pay out the income to the beneficiaries each year while they are infants to utilise their personal allowances and, if required, their basic rate band. This can be a very substantial advantage and can provide funds for the payment of school fees at little or no tax cost.

- If the beneficiaries *are* the children of the settlor, this advantage is not available because the income paid to or for the benefit of the children would be treated as the income of the settlor. However, it is possible by means of a bare trust to accumulate a substantial fund (tax free) for the benefit of the children on their 18th birthday.

- Where the children of the settlor are married or *over 18*, this rules does not apply and funds can be paid out to the beneficiaries, e.g. for the purposes of their university education. Such income is taxed as the income of the beneficiaries, against which their personal allowances can be set, and the balance is charged only at the basic rate of tax, subject to the other income of the beneficiary.

Trusts and Capital Gains Tax

Trustees are liable to capital gains tax on their own gains and are entitled to their own annual exemption, which is usually one-half of the exemption which applies to an individual. However, this does not apply where the settlor or his spouse has an interest under the settlement, because in that case the gains made by the trustees will be treated as the gains of the settlor and taxed accordingly.

Trustees are taxed on capital gains at a rate of 25 per cent only, unless any part of their income is chargeable to tax at 35 per cent, in which case this higher rate will apply to capital gains tax as well. Accordingly, an advantage can be obtained by putting assets into trust which would otherwise be chargeable to capital gains tax at 40 per cent on their disposal, because if the settlor does not have an interest under the settlement, the capital gains tax charge can be limited to 25 per cent only.

Any transfers of assets to trustees will be treated as disposals for capital gains tax purposes by the settlor. Usually, the assets will be transferred by way of gift, but will be treated for capital gains tax purposes as if they had been sold by the settlor at market value. Depending upon the value of the assets at the time of the transfer, this may give rise to a capital gains tax liability, subject to any reliefs or exemptions which may be available to the settlor. Some transfers of assets can benefit from a special relief – known as hold-over relief, i.e. the trustees can be treated as acquiring an asset at the original cost to the settlor so that the tax is deferred until the assets are sold by the trustees. A transfer of assets to a settlement will not usually be considered unless this relief is available, because the settlor will not want to create a tax liability on setting up the trust.

Clearly, it is advantageous to make early transfers of assets to a trust before any significant gain has arisen and this is particularly relevant to transfers to offshore (i.e. non-resident) trusts. This aspect is dealt with in Chapter 6.

When assets are distributed from a trust to the beneficiaries, this is regarded as a disposal at market value by the trustees for the purposes of capital gains tax and a charge to tax may therefore arise. So, care must be taken in planning such distributions if the settled property has grown in value significantly during the trustees' ownership.

A charge can also arise on the occasion when a beneficiary becomes absolutely entitled to part of the settled property. The trustees may be able to claim hold-over relief if the assets are of a suitable nature and there are other exemptions (such as the private residence exemption on a dwelling house occupied by a beneficiary) which may also be available.

Cash is not a chargeable asset and can be distributed to the beneficiaries free of capital gains tax.

Inheritance Tax

In the field of inheritance tax, trusts can give rise to considerable advantages. These are mainly by virtue of the separation which takes place between the legal ownership of the assets and those entitled to the benefit of the assets, and because of the differing entitlements to income and capital which can be created.

As a general principle, the person entitled to an interest in possession in the settled property (i.e. the right to the income as it arises) is treated for inheritance tax purposes as being beneficially entitled to the assets themselves. Therefore, a simple life interest settlement in favour of the settlor will not provide any inheritance tax saving for the settlor.

However, in many cases the settlor will not want to continue to receive the income from the assets – indeed, the assets may not give rise to any income. The settlor will often want to remove the assets from his estate for inheritance tax purposes, but without necessarily giving those assets to his children or anybody else – furthermore, he may want to keep them under his effective control. In these circumstances a trust can provide the complete answer.

He could, for example, transfer the assets to a discretionary trust for the benefit of his wife and family, thereby giving no entitlement to income to any other person, and the assets would be under the control of the trustees (of which he may be one). This is particularly helpful in the case of private company shares, where the continuity of voting control may be important. For this advantage to be obtained it is important to avoid the settlor reserving any benefit from the trust and this will be explained in detail in Chapter 7.

A transfer to a discretionary trust will be entirely satisfactory for gifts up to £147,000, but beyond that level inheritance tax arises at a rate of 20 per cent because such transfers are chargeable transfers for inheritance tax purposes.

This tax can be avoided by providing for the trust to confer an interest in possession on the beneficiaries giving them an entitlement to the income (if any) arising from the settled property, but with the settlor retaining the right to revoke the interest of the beneficiaries and to direct the property elsewhere if he wishes to do so. This would provide the settlor with the same degree of effective control over the assets as would exist under a discretionary settlement, but without any inheritance tax charge arising even if the assets involved exceed £147,000.

Shares in the Family Company

One particularly useful idea is to transfer assets to a discretionary trust which have a present value of less than £147,000, in the expectation that their value will increase substantially, for example shares in a family company which is expected to prosper. Quite apart from the capital gains tax advantage, such a transfer would give rise to no inheritance tax; it would be possible to rearrange the settlement within 10 years, perhaps by granting a life interest to a child or a contingent interest to grandchildren, without any charge to inheritance tax at all, whatever the value of the settled property at that time.

The almost infinite variety possible in the terms of a trust usually means that all the wishes of the settlor can be accommodated within its framework, while ensuring that the assets remain outside his estate for inheritance tax purposes. The choice of trustees and the opportunity to restrict the rights of the beneficiaries mean that the settlor need not lose control over the settled property, nor lose access to it in case of need for the benefit of his family. As you will see, trusts can be extremely useful when it comes to saving tax.

=5=

FAMILIES

Married Couples

Married couples have some extremely useful opportunities open to them for saving tax, simply by virtue of the fact that they are married. Leaving aside the obvious point that married couples obtain more personal allowances, an opportunity for income tax saving is available by making sure that you use both spouses' allowances and basic rate band, and that you double up on any tax advantageous investment opportunities. If both spouses have their own income and are both paying income at the top rate there is not a lot of scope, it is true. But there are still some worthwhile points to consider. However, in the case where one spouse is working and the other has no income, you can improve your situation considerably and save a good deal of tax.

Transferring Income between Spouses

The first point to remember is that since the introduction of independent taxation, husbands and wives are treated separately for tax purposes and each has their own personal allowance of £3,495; income up to that level will be tax free and the next £23,700 of income will be taxable at only 25 per cent. So, for example, if the husband is paying tax at 40 per cent on his salary, his investment income will also be taxed at that rate, whereas if the income were to belong to his wife, the tax would be very much lower. If the investment income, is, say, £10,000 per annum, a tax saving of £2,300 each year would arise, simply by arranging for the income to belong to the wife.

For this to be effective it is essential that the wife is entitled to the income, and there are further rules which are designed to prevent abuse. However, the rules are not really very tough and they only prevent arrangements whereby the wife becomes entitled to the income and not the capital – but you can get round that difficulty as well (see below 'Jointly Owned Assets'). Provided you give the income-producing assets to the wife absolutely, the income will be hers and will be taxed on her at her own rates. If you simply give her a right to income with no right to the underlying capital, it will not work.

Sale of Assets to Wife

The husband may not feel particularly inclined to transfer all his savings to his wife. If this is the case, one way to avoid increasing the wife's assets, while achieving the tax advantage, would be for the husband to sell his investments to her (possibly leaving the purchase price outstanding on loan if she does not have the money to pay for them), so that her wealth is not increased. The wife will then have the income-producing assets, and the income from them will be taxed on her.

Jointly Owned Assets

Another opportunity for tax saving arises if the spouses hold assets jointly. The tax rules treat any income arising from the investments as belonging to the spouses equally and each would therefore be taxed on half the income. This is particularly advantageous where one spouse wishes to transfer income to the other, but without parting with the underlying assets. A transfer into joint names, but with the beneficial ownership being 95 per cent to the husband and 5 per cent to the wife will do the trick.

Despite the wide disparity in beneficial ownership, the Inland Revenue will divide the income equally for tax purposes, unless the spouses elect to be taxed in accordance with their beneficial shares. So the husband keeps 95 per cent of the ownership of the investments, but enables the wife's lower rate of tax to be used against 50 per cent of the income.

Allocating the Mortgage Interest

Another election is available in respect of mortgage interest, because spouses can elect jointly to allocate the qualifying interest paid on their mortgage against the income of the spouse with the higher income, so as to maximise the benefit of the tax relief.

Partnerships

If you are in business you could decide to take your wife into partnership with you. This is an extremely valuable opportunity because the profits will be divided between you, thereby enabling the wife's allowances and basic rate tax band to be utilised. In Chapter 2, when we looked at the selection on accounting dates, it was explained how to create an advantage by admitting a new partner and that the choice of the date for the new partner to be taken into the business is extremely important. However, if this is to work it is essential that the Inland Revenue will accept that the wife is a genuine partner. It is unlikely that a wife who never attends the business premises and has no knowledge of the business will be regarded as a genuine partner in (say) a computer software design partnership, or perhaps a tax consultancy practice. However, that is not to say that she cannot be a partner in such a business; you just have to be careful with the arrangements.

A partnership is a relationship between two or more persons who carry on business in common with a view to making a profit. They do not need identical skills, but they do have to make a contribution to the business. Partners are equally liable for the debts of the business and, therefore, all decisions of the partnership of a substantial nature should be made jointly and should preferably be documented. Each partner should have signing rights to the bank account (and *both* should actually sign the cheques) and it should be made clear on the headed paper and invoices that they are both partners. A written partnership agreement setting out the terms of the partnership is useful, but only if it supports the facts; a partnership agreement on its own will have little evidential value in the case of a dispute with the Inland Revenue.

The wife need not work at the business premises, but she could work from home, writing up the books, sending out invoices, paying the bills or performing other functions which can conveniently be done from home, perhaps on the telephone.

The share of profits to which the partners are entitled can be relevant, but it is not good enough for the Inland Revenue simply to say that the wife's profit share is out of proportion to the services she provides. There are many partnerships where some partners are not worth their profit shares, but that does not prevent them from being genuine partners.

Your Spouse as a Sleeping Partner

Where the nature of the business, or perhaps the provision of the services, is such that a business partnership is not really a possibility, it is worth considering making your wife a limited, or sleeping, partner who contributes capital and little else. This would enable some advantage to be gained, if only to mop up her allowances if they cannot be used in another way.

Your Spouse as an Employee

For many other reasons it may be inappropriate or impossible for your wife to join you in partnership. One obvious example is where the business is carried on by a company. Whatever the reason it may be entirely reasonable for you to pay your wife a salary for her valuable work of assistance in the business. Such a salary would use up her allowances and her basic rate band and you would obtain a tax deduction in your business accounts for the amounts paid, provided they were a reasonable reward for the services performed by your wife.

In deciding what is a reasonable reward for your wife's services you should bear in mind that she would be required to work long and unsocial hours, often at weekends, in circumstances where it would be extremely difficult to recruit an employee. She also has an additional burden of being particularly nice to your clients or customers, because it will reflect badly on you otherwise. Your clients will not be prepared to accept the old excuse that it is difficult to get good staff these days! For these reasons the amount which may justifiably be paid to your wife could be a good deal higher than you imagine.

However, it is easy to go very wrong in paying a salary to your wife, because you need to take national insurance contributions into account and you can end up with a negative tax plan – i.e. how to arrange matters so that you pay more tax than if you did nothing.

For example:
Let us assume that a wife is paid £12,750 by her husband's business. She will pay tax of £2,364 calculated as under:

Income	Tax
£3445 (covered by her personal allowance)	–
£9305 @ 25%	2326
£12750	2326

Her earnings will also be liable to national insurance contributions and, on the above figures, NIC of £950 would be payable by the wife and £1,326 would be payable by the husband as her employer. This is a disaster, because you end up paying more in tax and national insurance contributions than you would if no salary had been paid. What needs to be done in these circumstances is for the salary to the wife to be limited to £2,750 so that no tax or national insurance contributions become payable. The husband will still be entitled to a tax deduction for the salary and an overall tax saving of up to £1,100 can be achieved.

Foreign Domiciled Spouses

If your wife is not UK domiciled, a whole vista of opportunity arises. The privileges attaching to foreign domiciled individuals have already been explained in Chapter 1, and obviously the UK domiciled spouse should make sure that their foreign domiciled spouse gets all the tax advantages which are going.

For example, a husband with a foreign domiciled wife should arrange for all his surplus funds to be transferred to his wife and for her to invest the money abroad. All the wife's foreign income will be taxable on the remittance basis and will therefore not be liable to UK tax unless and until the income is remitted to the UK.

If the couple actually need all the income from their savings this might be thought to be of no real benefit because they will have to remit the income to the UK to meet their living expenses. However, even in these circumstances it is possible for the money to be remitted in a way which does not give rise to any tax. There are three ways you can do this.

- The investments should be arranged so that there is a clear distinction between capital and income. For example, there may be a deposit account and a separate income account to which all income is credited. All remittances should therefore be made from the capital account and not from the income account. The remittances from the capital account are not income and are therefore not chargeable to income tax. If, however, the capital account might eventually run out, the wife could perhaps remit part of the income account each year sufficient to utilise her personal allowance.

- The income remitted will only be taxable if the source of the income is in existence during the tax year when the remittance of income takes place. Staying with the example of a foreign deposit account with a separate income account the source of the income (i.e. the deposit account) can be brought to an end by closing the deposit account shortly before 5 April in any year and transferring the whole lot to the UK after 5 April. (To avoid technical arguments with the Inland Revenue it is usually wise to ensure that both accounts are closed and all the money transferred to a new non-interest-bearing account with another bank.) In the subsequent tax year when the funds are remitted, the source will not exist and the whole of the amounts remitted will be tax free.

- It may be that neither of the above techniques is satisfactory. For example, the foreign assets may be investments which cannot easily be sold to enable remittances of capital to be made, or it may be inappropriate to terminate the source. There may just be a single bank account full of income which is wanted in the UK. If the wife needs the income you may think that she will have to pay tax on it. She cannot safely borrow against it because of the doctrine of 'constructive remittance', whereby the enjoyment of the income in the UK by a circuitous route will be treated as a remittance. However, what she can do is simply give the income to her husband by transferring the money to his bank account which must be outside the UK. This must be a genuine and outright gift, and the money must belong to the husband absolutely. (Particular care must be taken to make sure it is an effective gift because there is no presumption of advancement in favour of a transfer from a wife to a husband – unlike the other way round). As far as the husband is concerned the money is not income in his hands and he can therefore remit the whole of the money without any tax consequences. It is not a remittance by the wife nor even a constructive remittance; it is a remittance by the husband, but it is not income in his hands. Accordingly, the husband can have the whole of the income in the UK and no tax arises. He must keep the money himself, or spend it in a way that benefits him, because if the money is given back to the wife, or spent on her, the Inland Revenue could treat the whole arrangement as a sham and treat it as a taxable remittance by the wife.

Married Couples and Capital Gains Tax

Husbands and wives who are living together benefit from a valuable exemption from capital gains tax which is that any transfers between them will be treated as giving rise to no gain and no loss for capital gains tax purposes. What this means is that there is freedom to transfer assets between the spouses without any problems, to achieve the best tax position.

For example, if the husband has some shares which he would like to sell, but which would give rise to a gain of £11,000, he might be liable to capital gains tax of £2,080 after taking into account his annual exemption of £5,800. However, if he were to transfer half the shares to his wife, the transfer to the wife would give rise to no gain or loss. If they were both to sell their holdings, they would each be entitled to their own annual exemption and all the tax would be avoided.

It is, of course, essential that the gift is genuine. If this is going to work the shares transferred to the wife must belong to her and she must be free to sell them (or not) as she chooses. Again, she must also keep the proceeds or the Inland Revenue may well regard the whole thing as a sham and deny her the exemption.

This is a very useful means of maximising the capital gains tax exemptions, but the crucial point is that the spouses must be living together. A serious problem can arise if they become separated – quite apart from the fact that the husband may be disinclined to give assets to his wife if they are likely to become separated. Spouses are treated as connected persons for the purposes of capital gains tax and, generally, transfers of assets between connected persons are deemed to take place at market value with tax being charged accordingly. This rule does not apply to spouses who are living together, because the transfer is then treated as taking place at a price giving rise to no gain nor loss.

The difficulty arises if they separate and the husband transfers assets to the wife, perhaps the matrimonial home as part of the financial separation arrangements. They will still be married, and therefore connected persons, and the transaction will be treated for capital gains tax as a sale of the house at market value. Unfortunately, however, he does not gain the benefit of the spouse exemption because they are not living together. So the husband, in this case, can end up with a substantial tax liability instead of a tax saving.

Divorcing Couples

Where a couple are divorced there will usually be some discussion about the financial arrangements which often culminates in the payment by the husband to the wife of a lump sum or periodical payments. Since 1988, periodical payments are entirely tax free in the hands of the recipient and only a small tax deduction is available for the payer.

One of the key issues is usually the matrimonial home because, whoever owns it, the wife may want to remain in the house, probably with the children, and if the parties do not agree the courts will often make an order to this effect. If the husband retains an interest in the house he will continue to benefit from the private residence exemption until the house is ultimately sold and he obtains his share of the sale proceeds. However, he will only be entitled to this exemption if he does not have any other property on which he could claim the exemption. This places him in some difficulty, because he will want to buy another house to live in, but he will not be entitled to the capital gains tax exemption on both houses; he will only obtain the exemption on the new house. When the house which is occupied by the wife is ultimately sold he will pay capital gains tax, because he will only be entitled to the full exemption for a period of 3 years after he moves out. What he needs is a means by which he can obtain an exemption on the house occupied by the spouse, as well as the exemption on his own house.

The answer here is to use a trust. If the matrimonial home is transferred to a trust for the benefit of the husband and wife within 3 years of the separation, the transfer to the trust will not be chargeable to capital gains tax because it will benefit from the private residence exemption for both parties. The terms of the trust would be that the wife is entitled to occupy the property for the agreed period, for example until the children reach the age of 18. When the house is later sold, the trustees (for it is they who own the house) will be entitled to the capital gains tax exemption, because it will have been occupied throughout their period of ownership as the private residence of a person entitled to occupy it under the terms of the settlement. The fact that the husband may ultimately receive half the sale proceeds (or some other proportion) does not affect the matter and he will therefore receive his money free of capital gains tax. The husband would thus be provided with a tax exemption by his ex-wife's occupation of the property, notwithstanding that he has another house which qualifies for the relief.

Other methods by which a trust can be used to multiply the availability of the private residence exemption will be explained in Chapter 6.

Children

Some people, knowing that their children each have a personal allowance of £3,495, would like somehow to transfer income to the children and use up those allowances. There are, unfortunately, some extremely complicated tax rules to prevent you doing this. Where a parent invests money for a child, or gives it to the child to invest, the parent is taxed on the child's income. This is because the gift represents a settlement for tax purposes (a 'settlement' being defined as a disposition, trust, covenant, agreement, arrangement or transfer of assets) and the parent is a settlor of this settlement. Accordingly, any income paid to or for the benefit of the infant and unmarried child of the settlor is treated as the income of the settlor for all tax purposes. And that looks like being the end of that – except that there is a loophole.

Another practically hopeless alternative would be for the assets to be held in trust, perhaps contingently on the child reaching the age of 18 or marrying under that age. In these circumstances the income arising will be chargeable to basic rate tax, plus an additional rate of 10 per cent, giving tax of 35 per cent. This 35 per cent liability removes most, if not all, of the advantage of investing the money for the child. The trustees could pay out the income to or for the benefit of the infant child, but then the income would become taxable on the parent and further tax might arise.

Children's Investments

For these reasons, investments for children are confined conventionally to those producing little or no income, such as life policies, national savings certificates and possibly index-linked government securities. In recent years there have been various types of children's investments, the latest being a National Savings children's bonus bond, whereby an investment of up to £1,000 can be made for the infant child on which the yield will be tax free. This is all very well, but what is really required is a means of obtaining a much larger tax advantage, by using the children's tax allowances to shelter £3,445 of income for each child every year.

Using a Nominee

If you were to look at the legislation closely you would find that the rule whereby the income is taxed on the parent applies only where the income from the investment 'is paid to or for the benefit of the child'. This seems reasonably comprehensive because you might think that if the child's personal allowance is to be used, the child must actually receive the income. However, the important word is 'paid', because income can arise and belong to somebody without it actually being paid to them.

An example is an investment by a nominee for the absolute benefit of the child, with the income being retained and reinvested by the nominee. The nominee would be a bare trustee (as explained in Chapter 4), so that the underlying investment and the income would belong absolutely to the child. Because the income belongs to the child, but is not paid to the child or used for its benefit, the income is not treated as that of the parent, but remains the income of the child and covered by its own personal allowance.

The degree of advantage to be obtained from this idea depends upon the amount of income you can afford to divert to your children. If you can move income of £3,445, on which you would pay tax at 40 per cent, to each child who would pay no tax on it you will save tax of £1,378 each year per child.

You could go further, because beyond £3,445 the child would pay only 25 per cent tax and this is obviously better than the 40 per cent which you would otherwise pay.

However, it is important to remember that the idea is to build up a fund during the children's infancy, and you will pay income on any money paid to or for their benefit while they are under 18, and unmarried. This is not necessarily so serious, because if some money is needed for the child's benefit it can be paid out – the only point being that the amount paid out will be treated as the parents' income. The rest of the funds would not be affected and the tax you pay is only what you would have paid anyway.

Social consequences

Although this loophole can give rise to a large and continuing tax saving, you should not overlook the social consequences. Remember that the money belongs to the child absolutely, so when he is 18 and of legal capacity, he can call for it. The parent may have arranged for the money to be invested so that it is not immediately realisable, but the amount could still be very large, and therefore represent a problem.

There is clearly a balance to be struck here of obtaining a substantial tax saving without creating too large a fund for the child at age 18, which could cause other social difficulties to arise.

How to Make the Investment

The next point to consider is how the parent should make the investment for the child. Under no circumstances should any of the money be invested in the child's own name because the Inland Revenue take the view that this would represent payment to the child, thereby causing the income to be taxed on the parent.

One investment stratagem could be for the nominee to place the money in a national savings income bond (NSIB), which tends to pay income at a reasonable rate. The unusual feature of an NSIB is that it pays gross interest monthly and, if this income is paid direct to a national savings investment account (again in the name of the nominee), the income from the NSIB will generate further interest without deduction of tax. This would enable the funds to grow gross at a rapid rate, through the combination of the high rates of interest and the freedom of tax – and without any administrative involvement at all.

Once established, the funds can be left untouched for years – possibly until the child reaches the age of 18. Obviously it would be preferable for the investment to be reviewed periodically, if only perhaps to use some of the funds in the investment account to take some other investment opportunity which might generate a capital gain, bearing in mind that the child also has its own annual capital gains tax exemption.

Grandparents' Gifts

There is no reason why the above arrangements should not be made in exactly the same fashion with moneys derived from sources other than the parents of the child. Grandparents are the obvious alternative. This would make the arrangements vastly more effective because the income could then be paid out during infancy to or for the benefit of the child, (e.g. for holidays, clothing, school fees or anything else for his benefit), without forfeiting any of the income tax advantages.

This may have an added attraction, because it would avoid the possibility of the child becoming entitled to a disproportionately large sum on attaining the age of 18. By that age the fund could have been used to a significant extent for his education or benefit, leaving only the residue to see him through university or professional examinations.

===6===

CAPITAL GAINS TAX

What is Capital Gains Tax?

Capital gains tax is generally charged on profits made on capital assets, and is payable at the same rate that you would pay if the capital gains had been income. This does not mean that capital gains are treated as income; it is just a means of working out the tax you have to pay, so you cannot, for example, deduct personal allowances from a capital gain.

There are masses of exemptions and reliefs available in determining chargeable gains, and if you want to avoid the tax you could arrange matters so that you fall within a relief. Alternatively, you can find ways whereby your gain falls outside the scope of the tax completely. The effect would be the same; you would avoid the tax.

If neither of these avenues provides complete freedom from tax it is necessary to look carefully at how the gains are calculated because that can help you avoid some or all of the tax. In this chapter we will concentrate on all these areas.

It is unusual to find a receipt which is not going to be charged to income tax or capital gains tax; one of these taxes will nearly always apply when money comes into your hands. Some years ago when the highest rate of income tax was 98 per cent and the rate of capital gains tax was 30 per cent everybody tried like mad to obtain money as capital rather than as income. These efforts gave rise to a large body of tax law enabling the Inland Revenue to treat artificially created capital profits as income. However, now that the rates of tax for income and capital gains are the same, there is nothing like the same incentive to receive capital rather than income. It can still be advantageous, because indexation relief applies to capital gains and there is also an annual exemption for the first £5,800 of capital gains; neither of these reliefs apply for income tax. However, it will not always be advantageous to receive capital; there can be some substantial advantages in obtaining money in income form rather than capital and these are explained below.

Tax-Free Receipts

Most types of property, including assets and rights, are chargeable to capital gains tax. However some rights are simply not taxable at all, because for capital gains tax the rights must derive from an asset – if there is no asset there will be no capital gains tax. Generally, these are rights which have been provided by the law itself.

For example, if you have an agricultural or other tenancy and are protected by the Agricultural Holdings Act or the Landlord and Tenant Act, the statutory compensation you receive in the event of eviction is not chargeable to capital gains tax. This is not because it is specifically exempt from tax; it is because it does not derive from an asset. The Inland Revenue did not accept that such a loophole existed, but the courts have confirmed that it does and so far the Inland Revenue have not taken any steps to block the loophole. Unfortunately, such non-taxable rights are few and far between, but where they do exist the opportunity for tax-free receipt should not be overlooked.

There are other types of rights which, although they derive from assets, are specifically not chargeable to capital gains tax because the law says so. Examples would be betting winnings and damages for defamation – the more adventurous might see a loophole lurking here!

For example, somebody might want to buy your shares for £100,000 and you would rather not pay any tax. If he were to write a rude article about you and pay you £100,000 damages and then buy your shares for next to nothing, all would be well. Alternatively, you could play cards with him. You might win £100,000 and then he might win your shares. Wonderful! If you can convince the taxman that this is all true and bona fide it will work a treat. Personally, I would not even bother to try.

Selling 'Sets' of Articles

Other exemptions are provided as a matter of administrative convenience. Trivial gains which might take a long time to calculate and on which there may not be any tax at the end of the day are not cost-effective for the Inland Revenue to pursue.

For example, chattels such as furniture or bicycles would fall into this category and to prevent avoidance there is an overriding limit of £6,000 of sale proceeds. If you sell a piece of furniture or other tangible moveable property for less than £6,000, any gain you make is exempt from capital gains tax. By the same token any loss you may sustain on selling the asset would not be an allowable loss. You may, therefore, think that if you have a set of 12 chairs worth £18,000, you could sell each of them individually for £1,500 each and each one would be exempt. Unfortunately, it is not that simple because if you have a 'set' of articles and sell them off singly to the same person (or to a number of persons acting in concert), all the sales will be added together and tax will be charged accordingly. However, this does not close your opportunities completely. There is no definition of a set for this purpose and it would therefore be capable of being argued in all but the most obvious case that the relevant articles did not constitute a set.

The Inland Revenue seem to take the view that articles comprise a set if they would command a larger price than if they were sold individually. Apart from being illogical, this is a circular argument. There is no reason why an ordinary dinner service should not constitute a set, notwithstanding that it may be cheaper to buy the whole lot instead of the individual items separately. Where the articles themselves merely form a collection and have no intrinsic connection with each other, except that they are the same sort of thing (e.g. stamps), it can perhaps be argued that the individual items do not form a set.

More interesting is the position where there is a specifically designed set of articles, say five candelabra, and you only have four of them. You clearly do not have a set and a sale of all four separately might keep you outside the provisions.

Better still, particularly if you have in mind collecting all five of these candelabra from the outset knowing that they would together be worth a great deal, would be for you to create a different trust to acquire each one. Then the ownership of all five would be in separate hands and, although they would of course all be sold together to the same person to maximise the sale proceeds, the exemption would not be denied for each one. For most tax purposes connected persons (including trusts which you have established) are treated together, but strangely not for this provision.

Classic Motor Cars

Motor cars are another area of exemption. The law says that a capital gain made on the sale of a mechanically propelled road vehicle is exempt from capital gains tax. The reason is fairly simple; the Inland Revenue do not expect you to make a profit (you will probably make a loss), so it is cheaper for them to exempt all the gains because it will avoid them having to give an allowance for all the losses.

That is clear enough until you think of the situation with classic cars. If you buy a classic car, and sell it for twice as much in a year's time, the profit will be tax free by virtue of this exemption. Having regard to the enormous amounts of money which can be involved, the Inland Revenue are very keen to treat such transactions as a trade, in which case they will be chargeable to income tax, so great care must be taken to avoid trading treatment.

Annual Exemptions

Every person currently has an annual exemption of £5,800, which is the amount of capital gains which can be made in a single year without paying any capital gains tax. If you make a capital gain of more than £5,800 the first £5,800 is tax free. Unfortunately, unlike the inheritance tax annual exemption, you cannot carry this exemption forward from one year to another, and if you do not use it, you lose it. If you have a capital gain looming up of say £10,000, you will pay tax on the excess over £5,800, unless you can somehow use 2 years' exemptions against it.

What you need to do is to have two separate disposals in two separate tax years. If you are dealing with shares – you could sell half the shares in the first year and half the shares in the next year – but with other assets, such as a painting, for example it is a bit more difficult. It is absolutely no use arranging to be paid £5,000 in the first year and £5,000 in the next; that will not work at all. The methods by which a disposal may be divided into 2 tax years are explained in detail below.

Making Use of your Spouse's Annual Exemption

There may be another useful exemption, which is that available to your wife. If the asset is owned jointly by yourself and your wife any gain will be divided equally between you and you will each have your own annual exemption to set against the gain. If the asset is not in joint names of yourself and your wife, put it into joint names before it is sold and the exemptions will be allowed. But you must do this *before* the sale and not after the sale has been agreed. The gift to your wife must be genuine; you will be giving her half the asset and therefore half the sale proceeds. Provided you are happy with that, a gift to your wife immediately prior to the sale of an asset will enable her exemptions to be utilised. There is no capital gains tax or stamp duty on gifts between a husband and wife and this simple expedient can easily save £1,450 in capital gains tax, and possibly more, depending upon the size of the gain and the level of your wife's income.

And the Children

Remember that your children are individuals too and they have their own £5,800 capital gains tax exemption which may be going to waste. You may be able to give some assets pregnant with gain to your children and let them realise a £5,800 gain free of capital gains tax.

This is not as easy as a transaction with your spouse, because although a gift between spouses is exempt from capital gains tax, a gift to your children is not. Unless the assets qualify for a special holdover relief (see below), the transfer to the children will be treated as sale at market value and will create the very gain you are trying to avoid. However, provided you are dealing with a qualifying asset, such as shares in the family trading company, they can be given away freely because holdover relief will apply on the transfer to the children; they will be treated as acquiring the shares at your original cost or base value. This will enable them to realise a capital gain of their own and benefit from their own exemption.

If the assets do not qualify for holdover relief, for example if they are quoted shares, you will have to be a little more sophisticated. You could possibly transfer the shares into a discretionary trust and the trustees could later transfer the shares out of the trust to the children.

Unless you have a lot of children, this may not be worth while, but if you have two children (even if they are infants) and are able to arrange for the disposal for the assets to take place over 2 years, you have the opportunity of obtaining eight annual exemptions totalling £46,400, which could save you over £18,500 in tax.

It is essential to remember that the gifts to the children must be genuine and absolute. The sale proceeds will belong to the children absolutely and you cannot retrieve it for your own purposes. If the children are infants you are entitled to receive the money on their behalf as their parent or guardian, and are able to use the money for their maintenance, education and benefit during their infancy. (There is no aggregation rule for capital gains tax which causes the capital gains of infants to be treated as the gains of their parents.)

If you decide to do this you would be wise to take professional advice, not only to ensure that you deal with the money properly, but also to provide evidence to the Inland Revenue that the gifts to the children were genuine.

Bed and Breakfast Operations

Because the annual exemption only applies year by year it is sensible to make sure that you do not waste it. If you make no gains for 3 years, and then make gains of £15,000, you will pay capital gains tax on £9,200, whereas if you make gains of £5,000 in each of the 3 years you would pay no capital gains tax at all.

Unfortunately, it is not always convenient to make gains each year. You may have some shares which you want to keep for a long time because of their long-term growth potential, but you would still like to utilise your annual exemptions.

The way to get the best of both worlds is to do a bed and breakfast operation. What this means is that you sell just enough shares immediately before the end of the tax year to create a capital gain of £5,800 and then immediately buy the shares back again. In this way you effectively retain your original investment, but your base cost will be £5,800 higher than it was before and this will reduce the gain on the ultimate disposal. If you do this every year (and arrange for your spouse to do so as well), you can effectively increase the base cost of your shares by £11,600 each year, which can save a large amount of capital gains tax on the sale when you ultimately dispose of them.

The Importance of Timing

The time that you make your capital gain determines the date when you pay the tax. Capital gains are assessed on a tax year basis, so a capital gain made in the year ended 5 April 1992 will be assessed in 1991/2 and the tax will be payable on 1 December 1992. So if you want to dispose of an asset and make a large capital gain it will be worth while considering whether you can defer it until after the next 5 April. If you can, the tax will not be payable for a further 12 months and you will be able to hold on to the taxman's money for an extra year. That can be worth a good deal of money, depending upon the amount of the gain.

You may also want to defer the date of disposal until after the next 5 April, because you may be leaving the UK and want to make the disposal when you are neither resident nor ordinarily resident, and therefore outside the scope of capital gains tax. Alternatively, you may feel that it would be better to make the gain next year, so that you have a better opportunity in that year to reduce the tax by claiming other reliefs which may not be available this year. Or you may just want to pick up next year's annual exemption if you have used up this year's exemption – or you may want to use both.

It would be a simple matter to say to the purchaser that you do not want to sell the asset now but on 6 April next year, but he may not be prepared to wait and you may have no sale at all. What you need is a means by which you can do the deal now but have the sale treated as taking place next year.

When is the Date of Disposal?

It is essential to understand that the date of disposal for capital gains tax is the date when the contract is made, and not when the asset is conveyed or transferred. The date of payment does not matter – what matters is the contract date. So you must avoid entering into an agreement whereby you sell an asset now for say £100,000, with the proceeds being paid over 5 years. If you do this you will pay all the tax now, but you will not have the money for 5 years. If you ask them nicely, the Inland Revenue will give you time to pay the tax, but they will charge you interest on the unpaid tax which makes it rather expensive.

If you want to divide the sale between 2 tax years you could sell part of the asset in year 1 and the other part in year 2. You would not receive part of the sale proceeds until year 2, but you may feel that deferring the tax for the year would make that worth while. However, you need to watch out, because the purchaser may decide not to buy the second half in year 2; he may hit hard times or he may feel that having got the first half, he can do without the second half. If he is bound to buy the second half, you will have made a disposal of the whole lot in year 1 and no deferral will have been achieved.

Conditional Contracts

There are two main techniques you can use to deal with this situation. The first is the conditional contract. As mentioned above, the rule for capital gains tax is that the disposal takes place when the contract is made and not the time when the asset is conveyed or transferred. Where the contract is conditional the time of disposal is the date when the condition is satisfied.

A conditional contract can therefore bind both parties, but it does not come into effect until the condition is satisfied. The condition must be a condition precedent, e.g. the contract does not come into existence until the condition is satisfied, so provided the condition cannot be satisfied until the following 5 April, the deferral will be achieved. However, it must be more than simply fulfilling the terms of the contract. For example, a condition that the purchaser pays the money or that the subject matter remains in existence will not be a condition for this purpose. There has to be a contingency.

Granting the Purchaser an Option

Another means of deferring the effective date of disposal without placing yourself at risk is to grant the purchaser an option. What this means is that you sell the purchaser a right to purchase the asset at a specified price and time after the chosen date. The date will, of course, be some time after the following 5 April. He does not have to buy but he has the option to do so if he wishes.

You may say that this does not help very much, because he might decide not to exercise his option – he might simply let it lapse. To encourage him not to do so you could charge him rather a lot for the option. If you charge enough for the option he will be sure to exercise it because otherwise he will lose the money he paid for the option. If that is still not satisfactory you can have cross-options; he will have an option to purchase after 5 April at the specified price if he wants to buy and you would have an option to force him to buy at the same price if he decides not to do so. These are called 'put' and 'call' options – the purchaser's option is a call option (he can call for the property to be sold to him) and your option is called a put option (you can put the obligation on him to buy). In this way you can be sure that he will not back out and the sale will take place some time after 5 April.

You must take great care with the drafting of the options because if they are carelessly drawn the Inland Revenue could argue that they really represent a contract at the date the options were granted – not when they are exercised. That would, of course, defeat the whole purpose.

Indexation Relief

An adjustment for indexation is allowed to give relief from capital gains tax on pure inflationary gains. For example, if you buy an asset for £6,000 and sell it for £7,500 after 3 years you will obviously make a capital gain of £1,500. However, if inflation during those years was 25 per cent you will not have made a gain in real terms at all – your investment will merely have kept pace with inflation. It is therefore rather hard on you to pay tax on merely maintaining the value of your investment. Since 1982 there has been a special relief known as indexation relief which means that you can effectively increase your cost price to take account of inflation and only pay tax on the real gain.

In the above example the indexed cost of your £6,000 asset would be £7,500, so that no gain would arise and no tax would be payable. If however you sold the asset for only £7,000, the indexation relief would cause a loss to arise on this disposal and this loss can be set off against other gains you may make on other assets.

What this means is that you can create a loss (or at least a substantially uplifted base value) by utilising these rules.

For example:
Let us assume that there are three companies – a parent company A, its subsidiary B and B's subsidiary C. A subscribes for 1,000 shares in B and B subscribes for 1,000 shares in C. At some later date C pays a dividend of £1,000 to B and B pays a dividend of £1,000 to A. A then subscribes for another 1,000 shares in B and round you go again.

Each new subscription of shares increases the base value of the overall shareholding, but does not increase the value of the subsidiary, because the same amount of value is being removed each time by the payment of the dividend. At the end of the day when company B is sold or wound up, A will have an enormous base value which will reduce or eliminate the capital gain or produce a loss; the same applies to company B's shareholding in C. The money does seem to go round in a circle and for this reason a careful eye needs to be kept on the possibility of the Inland Revenue invoking *Furniss* v. *Dawson* (see Chapter 1), but there is nothing to prevent this arrangement being effective under the strict wording of the legislation.

1982 Rebasing

When calculating your capital gains you start off by taking the sale proceeds, less any expenses of sale, and deducting from the proceeds of sale the cost of acquiring the asset. If you bought the asset since 1982 the calculation is straightforward, but if you held it on 31 March 1982 you can substitute the March 1982 value so that you only pay tax on the increase in value since that date. You are still entitled to indexation relief so that you can take the 1982 value, uplift it by the retail price index since that date and only pay capital gains tax on the profit you make over and above this value.

Holdover Relief

Holdover Relief is a relief of enormous value and it is central to many techniques for saving capital gains tax, although its usefulness has been curtailed in recent years by restricting the relief only to certain classes of assets and transactions.

The reason why holdover relief exists in the first place is because capital gains tax is often charged on deemed disposals – that is to say where there is no real sale or no real disposal. An example would be a gift. If somebody gives you a valuable asset he is treated as disposing of it at market value and he pays capital gains tax as if he had sold the asset at market value. You are treated as if you bought it from him for cash equal to the market value. A claim for holdover relief displaces this deemed sale by treating your acquisition cost as the donor's original acquisition cost. When you sell the asset you will pay the tax on the whole of the gain. What this means is that you can move assets around without incurring any tax charge until such time as you find somebody with an exemption; they then realise the gain and no tax arises.

However, you cannot just give away an asset and claim to hold over the gain. The relief is restricted mainly to business assets and to transfers which are chargeable to inheritance tax. This means that gifts into discretionary settlements are eligible for holdover relief, even if they are too small in value to give rise to any inheritance tax, being below the nil rate threshold. Gifts to discretionary trusts beyond this level will give rise to inheritance tax at a rate of 20 per cent and therefore if the capital gains tax saving is large enough it could be worth paying a little bit of inheritance tax to save a great deal of capital gains tax.

Reducing the Rate of Capital Gains Tax

If the tax cannot be entirely avoided it is sometimes helpful to reduce the amount payable by arranging for the gain to be taxed at a lower rate. It has been explained above that the rate of capital gains tax is determined by reference to the size of your income, so with a capital gain of any size the rate of tax will obviously be 40 per cent. However, trustees of settlements which are not of a discretionary nature are liable to tax at the basic rate of 25 per cent only.

Accordingly, if you are about to make a large capital gain it would seem to be a good idea to transfer the asset to trustees who would make the gain, pay the reduced tax and then distribute all the proceeds to you. The Inland Revenue saw this particular loophole coming and where the settlor or his spouse has an interest under the settlement (that is to say if they are capable at some time of benefiting from the trust), all the gains of the trustees are deemed to accrue to the settlor; the gains are therefore chargeable at the settlor's rate of tax and not the reduced rate which would apply to the trustees.

However, where the settlor or his spouse do not have an interest under the settlement, for example where the children have life interests, the 25 per cent rate will apply to the gains made by the trustees, and a substantial saving can therefore be obtained.

119

Private Residences

There is a specific exemption for capital gains tax in respect of any gain you may make on your private residence, together with gardens up to $1/2$ hectare. You are only supposed to be entitled to the relief in respect of one house, so that if you have more than one house which you use as a residence you have to elect which house is to benefit from the exemption. To get the full exemption you have to use the house as your only or main residence throughout your period of ownership.

This seems straightforward enough, and you may think that there is not a lot of scope here for finding loopholes, but you would be wrong. Remember that wherever there is a relief there is always a possibility of using it beyond its apparent scope.

Moving House

If you wish to move and have difficulty selling your old house, you may worry that you will lose the exemption if you move out before it is sold. After all, if you move into your new house you will not be using your old house as your only or main residence. Fortunately, there is a relief which allows you up to 3 years to sell your old house after you have moved out without forfeiting any part of your exemption. So, during that 3-year period you will be able to have the exemption on your new house because you actually live in it, and also on the old house for a period of 3 years after you moved out.

More Than One House

This relief can be used to extra advantage if you have a holiday home, because you can obtain a lot more capital gains tax exemptions than the Inland Revenue intended.

> *For example:*
> Let us assume that you have a house in London and a holiday home in Devon, which you use occasionally for holiday

purposes. You will need to elect for one of the houses to be your main residence and therefore exempt from capital gains tax on sale. This can be a difficult decision because you will probably want to claim exemption on the house that you sell first. But you will also want to claim exemption on the house that will make the bigger gain, which will not necessarily be the same one. You may want to sell your holiday home and pay no tax on any gain, but you would not want to give up the exemption on your London house which may be very much more valuable and would give rise to a much larger gain when you sell it later.

What you can do in this case is to elect for your holiday home to be regarded as your main residence for a short period – say six months. After this you can change your election and claim that the exemption applies to the London house.

On the surface this may seem to get you nowhere, because you have gained six months' capital gains tax exemption on the holiday home, although you have lost six months' capital gains tax exemption on the London house. However, this overlooks the three-year rule. If the holiday home has at any time during your period of ownership been your private residence you are entitled to the exemption in respect of a proportion of the gain – the six months for which you claimed that it was your main residence, and because it had at some time been your main residence, to the last three years of ownership as well. So while you are only giving up six months' exemption on the London home, you are gaining three and a half years' exemption on the holiday home.

The private residence exemption is not confined to property in the UK, and the above would be equally effective if your holiday home was a chalet in Val d'Isere – provided that you used it for sufficient time so that it could reasonably be regarded as a residence.

Unwedded Bliss!

Married couples are only entitled to one private residence exemption, but those who share their lives unburdened by the rights and obligations of holy matrimony are not so restricted. Unmarried partners are each entitled to a private residence exemption and can therefore have two properties between them which benefit from the full exemption.

Exemptions on Two or More Residences

Is it possible to obtain the full exemption on two or more houses at the same time? It used to be possible to claim an exemption in respect of a private residence provided for a dependent relative, but this rule was abolished in 1988. However, there are still ways to obtain an exemption for a dependent relative or for anybody else for whom you wish to provide a residence, such as a child, a friend or perhaps a secret companion.

One way is to buy the other person the house and they could live in it and obtain the exemption. But you may not feel inclined to be that generous because relationships sometimes deteriorate. You may be happy for them to live in the house – which would be a good investment for you – but not to give them the whole of the house completely. In these circumstances it is possible to obtain relief for another house (or for a number of other houses if you have a number of people you wish to benefit) by the use of a trust.

There are special rules for properties held in trust. One reason for these rules is to allow the exemption to be preserved by a widow whose husband left her the house in trust during her lifetime. She would not own the house and would therefore not make the gain. The trustees would own the house, but they would not be occupying it. The conditions for the exemption are satisfied – but not all by the same person. So the law provides that where, throughout the period of ownership by the trustees, the house has been the main residence of a person entitled to occupy it under the terms of the trust, the trustees will be entitled to the private residence exemption on a sale.

If you have a friend for whom you wish to provide a house, you can create a trust to own the property and the friend could occupy it under the terms of the trust. The trustees could have power to terminate their occupation if they saw fit to do so and any gain made on the disposal would be eligible for the private residence exemption.

Taking this a stage further, you may have a holiday home which you have owned for a long time and you would like to do better than simply gain the exemption on the last 3 or 4 years of ownership in the manner described above. You want the whole of the gain to be exempt. Again, a trust can provide the answer.

For example:
You could transfer the holiday home to a trust (it would need to be a discretionary trust for the reasons explained when we were looking at the holdover relief, so as to avoid any capital gains on the transfer to the trust), and one of your children could occupy the house under the terms of the trust. The occupation would have to be for a reasonable period, after which it can be sold. Throughout the trustees' period of ownership it would be occupied by a person entitled to do so under the settlement and the whole gain would be exempt.

Because of the need to use a discretionary trust, a liability to inheritance tax could arise if the value of the property exceeded £150,000, or £300,000 if it were owned jointly by the husband and wife. However, these limits are sufficiently high not to cause a problem in most cases.

The Garden

Some houses have grounds or gardens of more than ¹/₂ hectare, but that does not necessarily mean that you will be liable to capital gains tax on the excess. The exemption extends to the garden or grounds up to ¹/₂ hectare, or such a large area as is required for the reasonable enjoyment of the house as a residence having regard to the size and character of the house. This is nice and vague, and gives lots of scope for negotiation.

You must, therefore, put yourself in the best position to claim that the largest area should be exempt. Do not fence part of it off or let it to a local farmer, because that would be good evidence that the fenced part was not required for the reasonable enjoyment of the house as a residence. Use the whole area if you can and take photographs of it showing that the whole of the surrounding land can reasonably be regarded as a garden. If the grounds are large (and out of keeping with the house) choose the largest possible area that can be regarded as garden, so as to maximise the part which will be exempt.

Selling the garden

If you sell off part of the land for development you may be faced with the argument that it was obviously not required for the reasonable enjoyment of the house or you could not have sold it off. However, that does not necessarily follow. You might well argue that the plot sold off was required for the reasonable use of the house, but you were prepared to restrict your enjoyment to an unreasonable degree, because you were amply compensated by the high price you received for the development plot.

What you must *never* do if you want to keep the exemption is to sell the house and keep a plot for later development. On a later sale it cannot be exempt under any circumstances and you will pay tax on it in full.

Let Properties

There is no limit to the number of trusts you can have for this purpose. If you have a portfolio of rented properties, there would seem to be no reason in principle why you should not transfer each property to a separate trust, with the tenant as the beneficiary. The trustees would allow the tenant to rent the property in accordance with the terms of the settlement and the whole property portfolio could therefore be exempt from capital gains tax. (Note that if the lack of holdover relief were to be a problem, a discretionary trust or a series of discretionary trusts would be necessary and inheritance tax would need to be considered in this context.) Every time the tenant changed, the trustees could exercise their power to appoint the new tenant as a beneficiary, and there would be no need to go to the trouble and expense of a new settlement on each change.

Of course the Inland Revenue might argue that when a property is let to a tenant at a market rent, the tenant would occupy the property under a contract with the trustees and not by reason of his or her interest under the settlement. To avoid any difficulties with this argument the terms of the settlement, and the arrangements with the occupier, must be framed in such a way as to ensure that the occupier's settlement arises by virtue of his position as beneficiary and not by virtue of the rental payments.

Business Use of the House

Some people use part of their house for the purposes of their business and claim a proportion of the running expenses as a tax deduction in their business accounts. This is a perfectly normal and conventional thing to do. However, it is sometimes suggested that this will cause part of the house to be chargeable to capital gains tax when it is sold. This derives from the rule which says that if part of the house is used *exclusively* for the purposes of the business, that proportion will not be eligible for the exemption.

The crucial word here is 'exclusively'. If you use part of the house exclusively for business purposes, e.g. if you are a dentist and your front room is your surgery, there is clearly a problem, but in most cases the business use will be far from exclusive. You may have a study when you work at home, but that would not mean that your study is exclusively used for your business. You would also use it for your own domestic purposes and the lack of exclusivity will mean that your capital gains tax exemption is wholly preserved.

The Inspector of Taxes may say that you can only claim for expenses if they are wholly and exclusively incurred for the purposes of the business. Although that is the strict rule, the Inland Revenue usually allows a proportion of the expenses to be claimed, and that has no bearing on whether the use of the part of the house is in fact 'exclusively' used for business purposes.

Job-Related Accommodation

Another means of obtaining the benefit of the private residence exemption is to qualify under the rules for job-related accommodation. You will be in job-related accommodation a) where you are provided with a house by your employer and it is necessary for you to live in the house for the proper performance of your duties, or b) if it is the kind of employment where it is customary for employers to provide living accommodation for their employees. If you buy another property yourself for holiday use, or perhaps for your use when you retire (or are dismissed), you are entitled to the capital gains tax exemption on the house, even if you never actually live in it. However, you must have intended at some time (any time will do – even if you later change your mind) to occupy it as your main residence.

It does not matter where the property is. It could be a holiday home in the sun, or the snow, and it could be let all the time. Provided you intended (at some time) to occupy it as your main residence, the exemption will apply and no tax will arise on any gain made on the sale.

It may be that you would have some difficulty in saying truthfully that your holiday home was intended to be your main residence eventually. You may be in secure employment and bought the house as an investment, intending to sell it and buy another to occupy in due course. This will preclude you from claiming the exemption under this special rule – but all is not lost. In these circumstances you should make sure that you actually use it for short periods each year for residential purposes. If you do, the property will be your residence – it will be your *only* residence – and so the exemption should be available anyway under general principles.

The Family Business

Selling the Business

A fairly typical problem facing many proprietors of a business is that in due course they will want to cash in on their success and sell the business at a large profit. In many cases there will be a valuable property from which the business is carried out. If you are over the age of 55 you may be able to obtain retirement relief to shelter part or all of the capital gain on the disposal, or you may want to start a new business and claim rollover relief by reinvesting all your sale proceeds into the new business. These reliefs are explained in more detail below. However, what do you do if you are too young for retirement relief and do not want to spend all the money on a new business, and you just want to sell the business and enjoy a gentle lifestyle?

You could simply sell all the assets including the property, get as much money as you can and pay capital gains tax on the gain after deducting indexation relief and your annual exemption. However, you may prefer to improve on this. The tax on such a disposal can be entirely avoided, with a little advance planning, by transferring the business to a new company in exchange for shares in that company. By doing so you would own all the shares in the company and the company would thereafter carry on the business. This has a number of income tax implications and the advantages which can be derived from incorporation of an existing business have already been explained in detail in Chapter 3.

Special relief on incorporation

As far as capital gains tax is concerned there is a special relief so that the transfer of the assets to the company in exchange for the shares will not give rise to any capital gains tax; what happens is that you are treated as acquiring shares in the company at your original base cost of the assets of the business. Effectively, this is a kind of rollover relief whereby your capital gains are rolled into the shares. When you ultimately sell the shares, the capital gain is calculated by reference to your original base cost of the business assets.

This may not seem like a particularly good idea because you have not obtained any money, or realised any gain. What you had in mind was selling the business. You now have a business being carried on by a company and you will pay the tax when you sell the shares to the purchaser. That is perfectly true, but you might decide not to sell the shares in the company, but to arrange for the company to sell the business assets instead. After all, that is what you were going to do before you incorporated the company and transferred the business to it.

The advantage lies in the price at which the assets are deemed to be acquired by the company. Whenever an asset is transferred between connected persons (and you and the company would certainly be connected for this purpose), the assets are deemed to be disposed of and acquired by the transferee at market value. No tax on this deemed disposal arises because of the special rollover relief into the shares, but that does affect the underlying principle that market value is deemed to apply to the transfer. Accordingly, the company is deemed to have acquired the assets at market value and if the company sells the assets before very long it will not make any capital gain – unless the assets have gone up in value in the interim, which is not very likely.

The result of doing this is that the company sells all the assets to the purchaser, receives all the money and pays no tax on the proceeds. If you later sell the shares or wind up the company capital gains tax will arise, but under the circumstances you would probably choose not to do so.

The company would have the whole of the sale proceeds in its hands tax free and these can be invested in any way that you see fit. The company would thereupon become your investment vehicle and because you own all the shares in the company it would make very little difference. The money in the company will usually represent savings which you would want to invest to provide an income in the long term and there is no reason why the company should not invest all the money in whatever way you choose to provide you with the income you require. You will obtain a much higher income, because you will be investing the tax saving as well.

It may be that you would want to carry on some part-time work or become involved in other businesses and the money in the company can quite properly be used for this purpose. Only if you really want the money out to spend in some manner which cannot or ought not to be undertaken by the company will you have to pay any tax.

It would, however, be preferable if as much money as possible could be paid to you tax free without interfering with your capital gains tax saving. When you transfer the business to the company it must be a transfer of a going concern and the whole of the assets of the business (other than cash) must be transferred to the company. The consideration for the transfer must be an issue to you of shares in the company. If the consideration is partly cash and partly shares, the part attributable to the cash will be chargeable to capital gains tax. If you have some reliefs, losses or other exemptions, you can thereby obtain some tax-free cash on the transfer, but in most cases this will not amount to a great deal.

However, any business carried on as a sole trader is usually financed by the proprietor's own money. You make profits and they are taxed each year and you draw money out of the business – but you cannot draw all the profits out because the business needs the money.

The result of this is that you build up a capital account. Look at your business accounts and you will find a section in the balance sheet entitled capital account. The balance on the capital account is your money which has been used to buy the assets shown on the other side of the balance sheet. If you, therefore, draw all this money out, possibly with the assistance of a bank overdraft, this money is yours on which tax has already been paid. You can then transfer all the assets of the business to the company and you will have stripped out a good deal of value from the business without damaging your capital gains tax advantage on the transfer. The company will need just as much money to carry on the business as it did before and you can then lend the money to the company. When the business is sold (or even if it is not), you can have this money back without any tax arising.

Family Company Shares

An area where capital gains tax frequently arises is in connection with the sale of shares in a family company. This is hardly surprising because many people, when they sell their family company, make a thumping gain. You may think that there is not much that can be done – after all you have your shares in the company, they cost (or the March 1982 value was) £x and indexation is, say, 75 per cent so that's that. But things are not quite that simple. You could, of course, just sell the shares and pay the tax, but you could do something else.

The purchaser may be interested in the company's business and be just as happy not to buy the shares from you, but to buy the assets from the company. Not all the assets will necessarily be chargeable assets giving rise to capital gains tax and furthermore the company may have the opportunity to claim rollover relief on any gains which are made, or other reliefs available to the company. This will be a simple alternative to a straightforward sale of the shares and may significantly reduce the tax payable. Some of the methods of exploiting rollover relief are explained below.

There may be assets in the company that you would prefer to keep, but it would be too expensive in tax to take them out of the company, so they all get sold with the company but not perhaps at the best price. For example, the company may own the premises from which the business is carried on. It may stretch the purchaser financially to acquire the premises as well and you will be much better selling him the business and keeping the premises, and selling them to somebody else at a better price, possibly renting them to him in the mean time. The alternative means of dealing with the sale are endless.

Before dealing with these points let us consider what can be done if you simply want to sell the shares. Immediately prior to the sale you could pay a large dividend to yourself and the other shareholders. The purchaser would naturally want to reduce the price he is paying for the shares if you are taking a large dividend and removing a great chunk of the company's assets, but that would not matter. You would be getting reduced sale proceeds from him and this would be compensated for by the dividend from the company. You may think that this achieves very little because you would pay tax at 40 per cent on the dividend and you would have paid 40 per cent on the profit on the shares. But do not overlook the tax credit which is available on a dividend.

For example:

If you were to reduce the purchase price by £150,000 and have a dividend of that amount instead, the capital gain would obviously go down by £150,000 and the dividend of £150,000 would be treated as taxable gross income of £200,000, from which £50,000 tax had been deducted. Although you would be liable to tax on the £200,000 at 40 per cent (which would be £80,000) you would be entitled to the tax credit of £50,000 to set against your income tax liability so that you would only have to pay £30,000.

Without any noticeable difference to yourself or the purchaser, you have substituted an income tax liability of £30,000 for the capital gains tax liability of £60,000.

When paying the dividend, the company has to pay advance corporation tax (ACT) of £50,000 to the Inland Revenue (it is this ACT which represents your tax credit), but the company will be able to set this ACT against its own corporation tax liability for the year (and if necessary carrying back the ACT for 6 years). The effect on the company would therefore be neutral, apart from the cash-flow effect of paying out the ACT and recovering it later from the Inland Revenue.

Retirement Relief

This technique can usefully be combined with retirement relief, which is a relief given from capital gains tax when you have been a full-time working director of your family trading company for 10 years and you dispose of your shares after you have reached the age of 55. The first £150,000 of gain is tax free and so is half of the next £450,000. (If you have not been a full-time working director for the last 10 years the relief is proportionately reduced.)

For example:

If you were to sell the shares for a gain of £1 million, you would be entitled to retirement relief of £375,000, and the balance of £625,000 would be liable to capital gains tax at 40 per cent – a liability of £250,000. If you were to have a dividend of £400,000 immediately before the sale and reduce the price, leaving a gain of £600,000, you would *still* receive maximum retirement relief of £375,000 and the capital gains tax would be reduced to 40 per cent of £225,000 which would be £90,000. You would, of course, pay income tax of £80,000 on the dividend making a total liability on the combined transactions of £170,000. This is £80,000 less than the tax you would otherwise have paid.

There is not much point in reducing the capital gain below £600,000 in this example, because if you are entitled to full retirement relief, the income tax on the dividend would be exactly the same as the capital gains tax on the profit.

Allowing the Company to Purchase its Own Shares

A variation on this theme is available if the person who wants to buy your shares is a fellow shareholder. Let us assume that the shares in the company are owned 50 per cent by yourself and 50 per cent by somebody else, and he wants to buy you out. A dividend would not be particularly attractive in these circumstances, because the dividend would be payable to all the shareholders and he may not find that convenient. Furthermore, although he might want to buy you out, he may have difficulty finding the money personally; it would be so much better to use the company's money for this purpose. In the circumstances you could arrange for the company itself to purchase your shares.

When a company purchases its own shares, the shares are cancelled. If your fellow shareholder had 50 per cent of the shares before the company's purchase, after the company's purchase and the cancellation of your shareholding, he will still have the same number of shares, but they will represent the whole of the issued share capital and his 50 per cent holding would therefore become 100 per cent. What is more, it is the company and not your fellow shareholder who pays the money and he therefore avoids burdening himself with a worrying degree of personal borrowings.

Capital or income?

A purchase by the company of its own shares can be arranged so that the amount you receive for your shares is treated as capital. You would therefore pay capital gains tax just as if you had sold the shares to a third party.

However, the purchase need not be done in that way. You can arrange for the purchase to be treated as a dividend, so that the amount you receive will be taxed as income and you will benefit from the tax credit, just as in the manner explained above. You will be liable to tax on the dividend at 40 per cent of the gross equivalent of the amount you receive, but you will be entitled to the 25 per cent tax credit. The effective rate of tax is therefore only 20 per cent of the amount you actually receive for the shares. This is obviously a much more attractive method of selling your shares to your fellow shareholder than him paying you direct. And he will no doubt think so too!

When your shares are purchased by the company they will be cancelled and, if you had originally paid anything to acquire them, you will obviously make a capital gains tax loss. You will receive nothing by way of capital for your shares – what you receive is treated as income and your original acquisition price (enhanced by indexation relief) will be your loss which can be set against any capital gains you may make in the same or any subsequent year.

As an alternative, if you had originally subscribed for the shares in the company, you could claim relief for the loss of your original subscription moneys as a deduction from your income. There is no reason why this loss cannot be set against the income you are treated as receiving on the purchase of your shares. If this income tax relief is not available you could divide the purchase and have part treated as capital, to absorb your capital loss, and the remainder treated as income in the manner referred to above.

An inheritance tax advantage

It can get better. It may be that the amounts you are going to receive for your shares are sufficiently high that you are considering giving some of the sale proceeds to your children as part of your inheritance tax planning arrangements. If you had in mind giving, say, £200,000 to your children for these reasons, this should be thought about more carefully. A better alternative would be to transfer £200,000 of these shares to a trust for your children so that they would be entitled to the income from the trust assets during their lifetime, and after their death the assets would pass to your grandchildren – with the trustees having power to advance all the money to your children absolutely if they thought it desirable. That would be a conventional life interest trust.

If the children were under the age of 18, a different type of trust would be required, but that does not affect the principle. Provided you and your spouse are wholly excluded from any benefit under this settlement, that part of the sale proceeds from the shares can, for all intents and purposes, be tax free.

How this works is that your transfer to the trust would give rise to no capital gains tax because you would be able to claim holdover relief on the transfer; the trustees would take over the shares for capital gains tax purposes at your base cost. The trustees would sell their shares to the company for £200,000 and, although it would be treated as income in the hands of the trustees, and taxable at the basic rate of tax, the basic rate would be entirely covered by the tax credit. Trustees are not liable to tax at the higher rate and therefore no further tax would be payable. If the trustees were liable to the additional rate which applies to some trusts, then a further liability would arise, but the type of trust referred to above would not be liable to this additional rate.

It might be thought that because the children are entitled to the income from the settlement and the amount received is treated as income for tax purposes, the children ought to pay tax at the higher rate on the amount of income attributable to them. However, although the sale proceeds would be treated as income as far as the trustees are concerned, it would not be income of the beneficiaries because it would be the sale of a capital asset and not distributable as income for trust law purposes. Accordingly, the £200,000 received on the sale of the shares would be subject to no further tax at all. Even when the trustees pay the £200,000 out to the children, there would be no tax liability. This may sound too good to be true, but it is a technique accepted as effective by the Inland Revenue.

Groups of companies

A further development of this idea relates to a group of companies where it is proposed to sell one of the subsidiaries. The situation will be fairly conventional. The family company A Ltd owns all the shares in a subsidiary B Ltd and the question is how do you sell B Ltd for, say, £1 million without any capital gains tax? All you need to do is to arrange for B Ltd to pay a dividend of £1 million to A Ltd and then sell its shares in B Ltd to the purchaser for £1. The important point here is that dividends from one UK company to another are tax free in the hands of the recipient and, furthermore, if the recipient owns 51 per cent of the company paying the dividend, an election can be made to pay the dividend without any advance corporation tax becoming payable as well.

How to Retire at the Same Time

Some people, when they sell the family company or business, decide to retire to the sun and become non-resident and in that case a different opportunity arises. They could sell up, pay the tax and then emigrate to their island paradise, but it would be so much better for them to leave first and sell the shares after they had safely established themselves as neither resident nor ordinarily resident in the UK, because then they would be outside the scope of capital gains tax and their sale proceeds would be free of tax.

This sounds as if it suffers from a fundamental practical difficulty because the business will probably collapse if they neglect it by leaving the company. However, what is needed is a deferral mechanism so that they can leave without producing an advantageous sale.

When we looked at the timing of capital tax disposals it was explained how a sale can be deferred for tax purposes, by use of a conditional contract or options. In these circumstances the purchaser may want to take over the business now, but you may not want to sell it until next year when you are safely settled abroad. Accordingly, you can grant him an option to buy your shares on some future date in the next tax year (and you can have an option forcing him to buy your shares if he decides not to exercise his option) and off you go. He can take over the running of the business and you are secure in the knowledge that, one way or another, you will receive your sale proceeds next year when you are non-resident.

You do, of course, need to take some care that the purchaser does not strip the company's assets and disappear in the other direction, but that can be dealt with by arranging for appropriate security to be provided.

It is, however, absolutely essential not to enter into arrangements which can be regarded as a binding contract before you leave – even an unwritten understanding about what will happen could be enough to create a binding contract. If such a contract is entered into before you go, the whole plan will be ruined because the date of disposal will be the date of the contract, which took place while you were UK resident and within the charge to capital gains tax. However, this point is unlikely to give rise to any difficulty if properly drawn options are prepared and understood by both parties.

This type of arrangement is not at all suitable if you do not intend to be away from the UK for long. If the only reason you are planning to leave the UK is to save tax, you have to be very careful indeed. The Inland Revenue will look at the circumstances very closely after your return and may well decide that you are not ordinarily resident abroad and therefore did not fall outside the scope of capital gains tax. This would obviously interfere rather substantially with your tax saving plan.

You should appreciate that when you go abroad the Inland Revenue will want to know where you are going and for how long, and although they will usually regard you as neither resident nor ordinarily resident from the day after your departure, or at the very least from the beginning of the next tax year, this would only be a provisional view and it will be reviewed later. If you come back in a year or two they might conclude you were not away long enough to establish ordinary residence abroad and charge your gain to capital gains tax.

You can argue, of course, but a protracted legal dispute (which you may lose – and even if you do not it will cost a lot of money in professional fees) is clearly something to be avoided. The concept of ordinary residence is difficult and opinions differ on how long you should be away, but to be safe you should be away for at least a complete tax year (and not return to the UK at any time during that tax year) and you should stay away (with only minimal visits to the UK if really necessary) for the 2 subsequent tax years. This can be extremely disruptive and inconvenient, and often makes going abroad in order to save tax a lot less attractive than is often supposed.

If, however, you are going genuinely to live abroad permanently and will not be resuming UK residence, there will be little danger in selling the shares in the tax year immediately following your departure, because even on a later review the Inland Revenue will not revise their provisional ruling on your residence.

Rollover Relief

Rollover relief is the colloquial term for a relief from capital gains tax where business assets are replaced. The idea is simple enough. If you sell an asset which you use for the purposes of your business and you spend all the proceeds in buying a replacement asset, you need not pay any capital gains tax on the sale of the old asset; you can roll over the gain into the new asset by deducting the amount of the gain from the base cost of the new asset.

The assets qualifying for this relief are in a fairly narrow category, mainly land and buildings, goodwill, and fixed plant and machinery (which means plant and machinery which is actually fixed to the floor), and there is a lengthy period, starting 1 year before the disposal and ending 3 years after the disposal, in which to buy the replacement asset. Capital gains tax is so full of deemed disposals and reliefs that the most surprising loopholes arise.

For example, let us assume that you have a business and you sell the whole business receiving £100,000 for the goodwill. To claim rollover relief you must reinvest the whole proceeds of sale in another qualifying asset used for the purposes of a trade. The new assets do not have to be used in the same trade – so you can set up another trade and roll over the gain into the qualifying assets of the new trade. This is helpful if you want to acquire another business, but this may not be what you had in mind. You may want the relief without actually spending the money. If your wife is in business you could purchase the business from her. That would not give rise to any capital gain in her hands because transfers of assets between spouses, even if paid for at full value, are treated as taking place at a price that gives rise to neither gain nor loss. However, you will still have spent the money on buying the business and there is no reason why you should not obtain rollover relief.

Groups and Subsidiaries

The same type of opportunity arises with a group of companies. If one company in a group makes a capital gain, you can transfer an asset around the group and claim rollover relief without any adverse tax consequences; transfers between companies in the same group are deemed to take place at a no gain/no loss value. In both the above examples all that has happened is that an asset has been transferred from the right hand to the left hand, but in a manner which provides entitlement to rollover relief.

This may not sound particularly helpful if you only have one company, because you would not have a group enabling you to make these transfers. However, there is nothing to stop you forming a subsidiary (thereby creating a group of companies), so that you will have the opportunity of making transfers qualifying for rollover relief.

Rearranging the Sale

If you carry on your business through a company a problem will arise if you simply sell the shares in the company at a capital gain. You may wish to sell the company and reinvest the proceeds in buying another company. Unfortunately, shares in companies are not qualifying assets for this purpose, so there is no possibility of a claim for rollover relief.

If, instead of selling your existing company, you arranged for the company to sell all its assets to the purchaser, the company would make a disposal of qualifying assets. The proceeds of sale could be used to purchase the shares in the new company. The new shares would not be qualifying assets, but if all the assets of the new company were then to be transferred to the original company, rollover relief would be available on the acquisition of those assets.

It is not *what* you do, but *how* you do it.

Gaining Retirement Relief

Another possibility also arises. Let us assume that you are 53 and propose to sell your business at a price which will give you a capital gain of £300,000. You want to retire, but you are too young to qualify for retirement relief which only applies (except in cases of genuine ill-health) in respect of sales over the age of 55. You could roll over the gain into a new business, but that is exactly what you do not want to do. You want to give up business and retire.

What you could do is to reinvest all the proceeds into property which is let as furnished holiday accommodation. Special rules apply to treat furnished holiday accommodation as a trade, so rollover relief would apply. After 2 years, when you reach the age of 55, you can sell the properties and claim retirement relief. Retirement relief gives a complete exemption up to £150,000 of gain and half of the next £450,000, so on your gain of £300,000 you would obtain retirement relief of £225,000, reducing your gain to £75,000. The tax saving by this manoeuvre would be £90,000.

Retrospective Planning

Because of the long period in which you have to reinvest the proceeds of sale to claim rollover relief, you can use the relief to repair the damage if you have made a capital gain on disposing of a business asset without giving the tax implications any consideration.

Let us assume that you sell your business and then think that it would be a good idea if you could save the tax. It sounds as if it is a bit late. What you should have done *before* you sold your business was to transfer the business to a company in exchange for shares (as I explained in Chapter 3). This would have enabled the company to sell the business assets without a charge to capital gains tax.

You cannot go back and start all over again, but what you can do is to buy another business, roll over your gain into this new business so you are back in the same position. Now you can transfer the business to a company in exchange for shares, so that the company can then sell the business assets without a charge to capital gains tax.

Foreign assets

If you have in mind selling your business and retiring abroad, it obviously makes sense to do a little tax planning in advance, so that the gain arises in a year in which you are neither resident nor ordinarily resident in the UK and outside the scope of capital gains tax. The ways in which this can be achieved were explained above. However, it may be that you do not get round to thinking about the tax implications until after the sale, by which time it is too late.

All may not be lost, however, because rollover relief can still come to your aid.

There is nothing to prevent you rolling over your gain into foreign assets. Therefore, the acquisition of replacement assets (or perhaps the purchase of a business) in the place where you plan to retire could enable you to roll over the original gain; on the later sale of the replacement asset no tax would arise, because by that time your non-residence would be secure.

Offshore Trusts

The History

Until March 1991 the use of non-resident trusts was wide-spread. Such trusts were extremely useful vehicles for avoiding capital gains tax, although they had little or no advantages for income tax and inheritance tax where entirely different rules apply.

In essence, the idea was that capital gains made by non-resident trustees are not chargeable to capital gains tax because the trustees are neither resident nor ordinarily resident in the UK, and outside the scope of the charge. The rule which applies to UK trusts that the trust gains are treated as the gains of the settlor did not apply to non-resident trusts; it does now. Although the capital gains made by the trustees were tax free in the hands of the trustees, the beneficiaries could still be charged to tax on those gains to the extent that they received 'capital payments' from the trust. A capital payment means not only a payment of money, but also the conferring of any other benefit so distributions from the trust to the beneficiary would be chargeable to capital gains tax in the hands of the beneficiaries. However, it was possible to reduce capital gains tax liabilities to negligible proportions by ensuring that the capital payments were of very low value. The purchase of an asset for the use of a beneficiary, or an interest-free loan, would certainly represent a benefit and therefore a capital payment, but the value of the benefit would not be the full cost of the asset or the amount of the loan; it would only be the value of the right to use the asset temporarily. The measure of the capital payment would therefore be comparatively small and the capital gains tax liability even smaller.

For these reasons a large number of people spent a great deal of time transferring assets into non-resident trusts, so as to shelter them from capital gains tax in the long term, safe in the knowledge that they could and would effectively enjoy the proceeds of any capital gains without any significant capital gains tax liabilities arising.

Unfortunately, but perhaps inevitably, these highly advantageous rules came to an end in March 1991 and the benefits from using non-resident trusts are now much more difficult to obtain. But the opportunities have not completely disappeared.

And now?

The main part of the new rules provide that if a UK trust becomes not resident, all the trust assets are deemed to be sold by the trustees and a capital gains tax liability then arises. This is called an 'exit charge' and effectively prevents trusts with assets pregnant with gains from being exported to realise the gains tax free. However, if the amounts in the trust are not particularly valuable at the moment, but are expected to grow in value in due course, an exit charge would give rise to little or no tax and the trust could therefore be exported without any significant tax penalty.

The second element of the new rules is that if the settlor has an interest in the settlement (which means if the settlor or his spouse, or his children or their spouses can benefit), all the gains made by the non-resident trustees will be treated as the capital gains of the settlor and taxed accordingly. This is called the see-through provision.

However, brothers and sisters are not included in the list, nor are parents or grandchildren. So, if a grandparent wishes to set up a trust for a grandchild, it would be very sensible to establish a non-resident trust so that the whole fund will be free from capital gains tax and subject to the old rules, which means that any capital gains made by the trustees will be taxed only if and when the grandchildren receive capital payments.

Also, a non-resident trust set up by will is completely outside the new provisions. The assets will go into the trust at probate value and no exit charge will arise, and there will obviously be no possibility of the deceased enjoying any interest under the settlement.

Another possibility for reducing the exit charge would be to fragment the shareholdings in the trust. Instead of having one trust holding say, 60 per cent of the family company shares, you set up 5 separate trusts with 12 per cent of the shares each, you could then export one of the trusts. There will be a tax charge on the value of the 12 per cent shareholding, but such a small shareholding would not be valued very highly no matter how large the company, and the exit charge would be very small. You can then do this five times so that all the shares are effectively exported. This will not help very much if the settlor retained an interest under the settlement, but if he did not do so if, e.g. the settlement was established by a grandparent or by a deceased parent, brother or sister, or even a common-law wife, the new rules would not interfere with these arrangements at all.

Apart from the exit charge the new code for the taxation of non-resident trusts does not apply to non-domiciled individuals who continue to have freedom to establish such trusts and enjoy all capital gains in the UK without any possibility of a tax charge arising.

=7=

INHERITANCE TAX

The Problem

Inheritance tax is the latest name for death duties. It is charge-able on the value of your estate at your death and the rates change regularly. At the present time the first £147,000 is free of tax and everything above that level is charged at a flat rate of 40 per cent. If you make a gift during your lifetime it is usually regarded as a potentially exempt transfer, which means that it is exempt provided you survive for 7 years. However, if you die *within* 7 years, the value of the gift is brought into account and charged to tax on your death.

There are other types of transfers which are wholly exempt, and some which are chargeable even during your lifetime. These are all explained in more detail below.

In simple terms you are either going to keep your money until you die, in which case tax will be paid on it, or you are going to give it away during your lifetime. There is a third alternative which is that you can spend it all, so that there is nothing left by the time you die. The problem is that most people want to keep their hands on all their money. They do not want to spend it all because they might need it in later life when inflation and ill-health could conspire to leave them in financial difficulties. Some people who have plenty of money and will certainly not need it all, still want to keep control of it and not give it away to children whom they may not regard as worthy or appropriate

145

recipients. However, they still do not want to pay the tax if they can avoid it.

The essence of successful inheritance planning is to save the tax without actually giving anything away – or at least to make gifts without losing control of the assets, or necessarily putting them in the hands of somebody else.

For many people inheritance tax will be the largest liability they (or their families) will ever face. This is because the tax is charged on the *full* value of a person's assets at the time of his death, and even those of comparatively modest means may be storing up a possibly overwhelming liability. Take, for example, a husband and wife of 65 years of age, who are enjoying their mortgage-free retirement. Let us assume that they live in a house worth £250,000 and have savings of £150,000 to supplement an otherwise adequate pension. It would be entirely normal for their wills to provide everything to pass to the surviving spouse on the first death, so as to avoid any inheritance tax liability. They may rightly feel that their financial circumstances do not permit them to make substantial gifts to their children during their lifetimes, and just resign themselves to the fact that tax will have to be paid on their deaths.

However, they may not readily appreciate that the tax liability would, on these figures, amount to approximately £100,000 and substantially erode their life savings. Where the value does not comprise easily realisable investments, but for example property, it may be that the tax liability arising on the deaths simply cannot be paid without selling the property – possibly at a significant loss. For those with larger estates, the problems become correspondingly higher.

It is with these circumstances that this chapter is concerned. Careful planning can often enable most, if not all, of the inheritance tax liability to be eliminated, thereby preserving the family's wealth for the next generation. This is obviously a subject deserving a good deal of attention. The large amounts involved naturally give rise to complex rules, and some complication is therefore inevitable. This should not be a deterrent because, with care and patience, very substantial savings indeed can be achieved. Even if you yourself will not be around to see the fruits of your labours in reducing your inheritance tax liability, your family will be extremely appreciative and admire the skilled manner in which your property has been protected from the clutches of the Inland Revenue.

Trusts

Trusts have a very important part to play in inheritance tax planning. Many people are put off by the complexity and mystery of trusts, and it is true that they are complex and intellectually demanding. I have already given a brief introduction to trusts and their uses in connection with tax in Chapter 4.

What a trust does is enable you to segregate the three important elements in owning property: control over the property; entitlement to the capital; and entitlement to the income. The trustees have control over the property, so you must make sure that they are persons who can be trusted to act sensibly in a way you would like. You can say who gets the capital and who gets the income. It is this separation that gives rise to enormous advantages in connection with the determination of tax liabilities and, in particular, inheritance tax.

For example, say that you have a valuable family company and you want to remain in control of it. This is a perfectly reasonable wish; it is your company and you do not want anybody else having power to interfere – even (or possibly especially) your children. You may want to continue doing work in any way you want, draw a salary and receive dividends. However, you may prefer that the value of the company's shares are not chargeable to tax on your death. You can put the shares into a trust and remove the value from your estate without affecting your right to obtain income from the company and without losing control over the company.

The variations on this theme of having your cake and eating it are explained in the following pages.

Reserving a Benefit

The first concept to understand is that of the reserved benefit. If you make a gift and reserve a benefit from the asset given away, the gift will be ineffective, because the asset will be treated as remaining in your estate for inheritance tax purposes. This point is central to *all* inheritance tax planning. A gift is regarded as subject to a reservation of a benefit if the donee (the person to whom you give the gift) does not assume possession and enjoyment of the asset or if the donor is not wholly excluded from benefit from the asset. (The precise rules say 'virtually to the entire exclusion' from any benefit, but nobody knows what this means, so it is dangerous to have any benefit from the asset at all.) It is not enough for you to cease to receive any benefit from the assets; if you are capable of obtaining a benefit you will not have been excluded from benefit, and the gift will be ineffective. You must be totally and irrevocably excluded from benefit.

An obvious example of this is your house. If you give away your house to your son, but continue to live in it as his guest, you will achieve no inheritance tax advantage, because your continued enjoyment of the property will be the reservation of a benefit.

An interesting feature of this rule is that, although the reservation of benefit by the donor will nullify the gift, the reservation of benefit for the donor's spouse does not do so. This gives rise to a substantial opportunity for inheritance tax saving, which is explained in detail below.

Shares – Avoiding Reservation of Benefits

The problem with the concept of reservations of benefits is that it is extremely wide and subtle. If, for example, you give away shares in your family company to your children, you may say that there is no reservation of a benefit. They have the shares, including all the voting rights, and are entitled to the dividends, so what have you retained?

Unfortunately the Inland Revenue take the view that if you remain employed by the company, enjoying a salary, that is a continuing benefit and the gift is ineffective. You may well say that this argument is misconceived. Your benefit comes from the company, not from the shares and many people would sympathise with this view. However, the Inland Revenue do have some decided cases in their favour and it is therefore wise to take precautions to avoid the problem.

What you should do instead is to have a service contract with the company to provide you with a salary, so that when you give the shares away, the company is already subject to the obligations from your contract of employment. Your entitlement to continued employment and salary is therefore dependent upon your contract with the company and wholly unconnected with, or reliant on, the shares given away.

Houses – A Shearing Operation

A variation on this theme can be adopted in connection with your house. If you would like to give away your house to your children and remain living in it, that would obviously be a reservation of a benefit. What you have to do is to separate the value of the house from your right to occupy it.

The way to do this is to grant a lease of the property to your wife (or to you both jointly) in which case two interests in the property will arise; you will have the freehold interest and your wife (or you and your wife jointly) will have the leasehold interest. You can then give away the freehold to your children. You will have no further interest in, or benefit from, the freehold. What you will have retained is the lease, which is an entirely separate asset giving you the right to occupy the property, probably at a nominal rent. The lease has to be long enough to ensure that it does not come to an end in your lifetime, because if it does, and you remain in occupation, a benefit will arise and you will be back to square one. Naturally, a lease of reasonable length at a nominal rent will be valuable, but a lot less valuable than the freehold house. What you had was a freehold house which was going up in value all the time; you now have much less valuable leasehold interest which is going down in value all the time.

While this can save a large amount of tax, it is not at all desirable if you think you might like to move house. If a move is planned or anticipated, these arrangements should be deferred until you have acquired your new home.

Spouses

It is well known that gifts during lifetime and on death to the surviving spouse are totally exempt from inheritance tax. So the easiest way to avoid inheritance tax is leave everything to your spouse.

This is not usually much of a solution because you just give the spouse a much bigger problem and probably less time in which to solve it. Furthermore, the first £147,000 of your estate is free from inheritance tax anyway, whoever you give it to, so leaving it to your spouse would waste that opportunity.

You should therefore consider leaving £147,000 to your children or anybody else you like, and leaving the rest to the surviving spouse.

However, you may not find that attractive because for example your spouse might need the money. What you need is a means whereby your spouse can have all the income and all the capital if necessary, but without giving rise to any tax on your death, or increasing your wife's estate. The answer is to transfer this £147,000 to a discretionary trust for the benefit of your wife and family. The trustees can ensure that your wife is properly provided for by paying money to her whenever she needs it, but the funds will remain under the control of your trustees and not in the hands of anybody else. This would have an added attraction if your wife is one of the trustees. At an inheritance tax rate of 40 per cent this will save tax of £58,800 by keeping the assets outside your wife's taxable estate, and could save another £58,800 if you set it up 7 years before your death.

Because you do not know which spouse is going to die first it is essential to ensure that both spouses have at least £147,000 in their estate. There is no point in going further than this because the tax is at a flat rate of 40 per cent over £147,000 anyway. Provided the spouse has at least £147,000, they can leave it on discretionary trusts for the benefit of the survivor, and fully utilise their nil rate band.

Foreign Spouses

If you are domiciled in the UK but your spouse is not, you have a problem because in these circumstances the total exemption between husband and wife does not exist. There is a limited exemption of only £55,000 if the transferee spouse is not UK domiciled – everything else is taxed as normal. This is not something you can afford to ignore because it will not go away, inflation will make it worse and it will be your spouse who has to pick up the pieces and pay the tax which could eliminate most or all of your savings and create financial difficulty.

However, although the loss of the spouse exemption is regrettable, if you understand the reasons why, you will see a huge opportunity for saving tax. Individuals domiciled in the UK are chargeable to inheritance tax on their worldwide assets, but foreign domiciled individuals are chargeable only on assets which are situated in the UK; all their foreign assets are excluded from the charge. So, if you have a foreign domiciled spouse, it makes a lot of sense to give all your assets to her and for her to place them abroad. They would then be immediately outside the scope of inheritance tax.

It is for this reason that there is a limited spouse exemption. However, this rule was created before the introduction of potentially exempt transfers and a loophole therefore exists in respect of lifetime gifts. A gift to your spouse during your lifetime would be treated the same as a gift to anybody else; it would be a potentially exempt transfer and, providing you survive for 7 years, the gift will be completely exempt. No tax would have arisen on the transfer of the assets to the spouse, no tax would arise on her transfer of the assets out of the country and no tax would arise on her death because the assets would be situated abroad. The Inland Revenue would know what you had done, but they will not cause any difficulty because you are merely playing by the rules.

If you are going to take advantage of this opportunity, you have to understand how to transfer assets abroad. Unfortunately it is not possible to put all your share certificates, bank statements and deeds of the house into a big bag, fly off to the Channel Islands and put it all in a safety deposit box. The rules are a little more sophisticated than that. Bank deposits can easily be transferred to a foreign branch of your normal bank, but moving the share certificates does not move the shares. Shares in private companies are regarded as situated in a country where the share register is located and you cannot move that. It is also a bit difficult with land.

What you can do is to transfer the shares to a Jersey company under your control. (This will represent a disposal for capital gains tax and you need to take care to ensure that no capital gains tax arises on this transfer.) For the same reason, the shares in the Jersey company will be regarded as being situated in Jersey. So, instead of owning your investments, you now own all the shares in the Jersey company which owns all of the investments. The big advantage is that the Jersey company's shares are outside the UK and are therefore not chargeable to inheritance tax if held by somebody who is not UK domiciled. Even better is the fact that this is effective from the moment you have done it and there is no need to wait 7 years.

Avoiding Reservation of Benefits through your Spouse

The existence of a spouse, even a UK domiciled spouse, provides advantages for other loopholes to be used.

For example:

Let us assume that you have a painting worth £100,000 which does not qualify for any particular exemption. You would like to avoid liability to inheritance tax on this £100,000, but you would also like to keep the painting on your wall. Your continued enjoyment of the painting would obviously be a reservation of benefit and the painting would be treated as remaining in your estate, even if you were to give it away. You need a loophole whereby you can remove the value of the painting from your estate, without depriving yourself of its enjoyment. This sounds like a contradiction in terms.

You could give the painting to your wife because the reservation of benefits provision do not apply to gifts between spouses. But that only shifts the problem sideways, because then she would have to remove it from her estate.

However, if you were to put the painting into a trust for the benefit of your wife for a period of (say) 1 year, after which date the trustees would have power to terminate her interest and transfer the painting to discretionary trusts for the benefit of the whole family, including yourself, it could stay on your wall without it forming part of your estate. You would obviously be enjoying the painting, but the reservation of benefit provisions would not apply to you. This is for the highly technical reason that the reservation of benefit provisions are contained in s. 102 of the Finance Act 1986. But s. 102(5)(*a*) says that the section does not apply if the gift is exempt because of the spouse exemption. So, if your gift benefits from the spouse exemption, you are outside the reservation of benefit regime and you can enjoy the painting to your heart's content. The only gift you make is the gift into the trust for the benefit of your wife. You do not make any further gift. After 1 year it stops being held for your wife and passes into discretionary trust; this will represent a chargeable transfer by your wife, but at a value of £100,000 no tax would arise, as it falls within her nil rate band. She would not be affected by the reservation of benefit rules, because she has not made a gift. She has done nothing, nor had any power to do anything, and it cannot be said that she has made a gift. You have not made a gift either, because your gift was to the trustees and that was exempt.

The result is that by directing a gift in this way, you get round the reservation of benefits provisions – although you will need expert help in preparing the necessary documents. This loophole can obviously be exploited in connection with any type of asset, not just your painting.

It will be appreciated that this loophole applies where the gift to the spouse is exempt, so it is obviously of only limited application where the transferee spouse is not domiciled in the UK. A gift of more than £55,000 would not be protected by s. 102(5)(*a*) and the excess would remain subject to the reservation of benefits rules. If both spouses are not UK domiciled, the unlimited exemption applies, but in those circumstances there would be little need to rely on this technique.

Discretionary Trusts for Your Spouse

A less complicated (and less controversial) arrangement would simply be to give £147,000 of your assets to a discretionary trust for the benefit of your wife and family. You must be excluded totally from any benefit under this settlement. However, there is no reason why your wife cannot be a beneficiary, so if you were ever to need the money it can be paid to her and she can use it for the relevant purpose. The money should not find its way back to you, it should be spent by your wife in accordance with her own wishes, but it may be reasonable to suppose that her wishes would coincide with your own. (Indeed the trustees, being wise custodians of the money, would probably not want to distribute anything to your wife if by doing so they were going to create conflict between the two of you.) What this will have achieved is effectively an inheritance tax-free money box capable of being raided by your wife. It will represent a chargeable transfer, i.e. one on which inheritance tax would be payable, but provided the amount put into the discretionary trust does not exceed the nil rate band, no inheritance tax would arise. After 7 years it would no longer be counted and you can do it again.

It must be appreciated that this is a device for avoiding inheritance tax and it has no effect at all on income tax and capital gains tax. These taxes will continue to apply unchanged as if nothing had been done at all.

Related Property

While we are on the subject of spouses, there is the question of related property to consider. This is a special rule which says that you must add together the property in the estates of the husband and wife for the purpose of determining the value of their respective assets. A simple example would be a pair of valuable earrings. They are only valuable as a pair and if you only had one it would hardly be worth anything. Therefore, if the husband owned one earring and the wife owned the other, the estate of each spouse would contain very little value. However, in reality if the earrings were to be sold they would be sold as a pair by both spouses. The tax rules provide for property comprised in the estate of the other spouse to be known as 'related property', so that it is valued together and then divided between the parties. Accordingly, in this example, the total value of the earrings as a pair would be calculated and each earring would be treated as being worth half of the total value.

The same principle applies to a company's shares. If a husband and wife each have 30 per cent of a company's shares, they each have a minority holding and the value of a 30 per cent holding is obviously a good deal less than half the value of a 60 per cent holding which carries control. The principle of related property applies to say that the value of each shareholding will be half the value of the combined holding.

This rule can be turned on its head and used to great advantage to devalue a husband's shareholding without incurring a charge to tax. As a first step you could arrange for your wife to have a small, say 2 per cent, shareholding in your company and then make various gifts yourself, possibly into trust, to your family so as to reduce your own shareholding down to 49 per cent. However, because of the related property rules your holding would be aggregated with that of your wife for the purposes of valuation, so your shareholding will still be valued on the assumption that it carried 51 per cent control. But your wife could give away her shares. Her 2 per cent holding would also be valued as part of a controlling holding, but as her shareholding is so small it would not matter. By disposing of her shares, she would prevent your shares from being valued as a controlling holding and her gift will have the effect of substantially devaluing your shares for the purposes of inheritance tax. There is no provision which enables this reduction in your estate to be chargeable to inheritance tax.

For example:
If we assume that a 51 per cent shareholding is worth £510,000, but a 49 per cent shareholding is worth only £350,000, a gift by the wife of her 2 per cent of the shares would be a transfer of only £20,000. However, the value of the husband's shares would go down from £490,000 to £350,000 without any charge to tax; nor would there be any need to wait for 7 years, because there is no transfer being made by the husband.

Tax-Advantageous Transfers to Charity

Another possibility would be for the majority shareholder to make gifts to bring his shareholding down to 51 per cent and then give 2 per cent to a charity. The same considerations would apply. His remaining shareholding would be dramatically reduced by much more than the mere 2 per cent gift, but because gifts to charities are exempt, no tax would arise. You may not fancy giving part of your shares to a charity, but having regard to the enormous potential tax saving it is worth while considering a very small transfer.

It becomes even more attractive if the charity is one of your own creation. If you set up your own charity you can be sure that you will not have any unwelcome interference from the charitable trustees. However, it must be appreciated that the Charity Commission and the Inland Revenue look at charities very closely indeed and will refuse to grant charitable status, unless they can be sure that it is bona fide established for charitable purposes. Accordingly, it will be necessary for the charity to have more than just a nominal shareholding in a private company which gives rise to no significant benefit to them. They should derive some positive benefit from the shares, such as a dividend which can be used for proper charitable purposes. This is obviously not difficult to arrange.

Note: Any attempt to use the charitable funds for any purposes other than bona fide charitable ones will cause the Inland Revenue to deny all the advantages you seek to achieve.

Fragmentation

Shares in a family company are frequently the subject of inheritance tax problems and it comes as no great surprise that loopholes are sought to enable shares to pass to the next generation without any significant charge to inheritance tax.

This particular loophole is a little more technical. If you own, say, 70 per cent of the shares in your family company, it will be clear from the previous paragraphs that this would be valued as a controlling holding, enabling you to get your own way on most matters. It will therefore be very much more valuable than, for example, seven times a 10 per cent holding. You could give 10 per cent away, but the gift would not be valued at the miserable value which would attach to a 10 per cent holding on its own – it would be valued at approximately one-seventh of a 70 per cent holding. The principle is known as the loss to the donor. You work out the value of a 70 per cent shareholding, then you work out what a 60 per cent shareholding would be worth and the value of the gift is the difference.

What you need to find is a means of avoiding this rule so that the shares can be valued in isolation. You could put 10 per cent of the shares in trust for your own benefit and after your death to your children, but this would achieve nothing, because you would still be treated as owning all the shares in the trust.

If, during your lifetime, the trustees were to transfer this 10 per cent to your children, you might expect the position to be exactly the same when it comes to valuing the shares. However, because of a loophole the rules do not work quite like that. What the rules say is that in these circumstances you are treated as making a gift, but that the value of the gift is the value of the property in the trust. The trust only has 10 per cent of the shares and there is nothing to attribute your shares to the trustees for the purposes of valuation or anything else. (Unfortunately this is not the case the other way round.) Accordingly, the value of the gift will be the value of a 10 per cent holding on its own, and that will obviously be very small.

Taking this a little further, if you were to divide your 70 per cent shareholding into seven separate trusts and did this operation seven times, the total value of the gifts would be only a small fraction of the total value of your holding. The fragmentation will have caused an enormous amount of value to fall out of your estate without any charge to tax.

The Inland Revenue were for a long time unwilling to accept this interpretation, but they have now agreed that it is correct. Their only argument is to suggest that the arrangements represent a preordained series of transactions so that the *Ramsay* doctrine (see Chapter 1) can be applied to disregard the transfers into and out of the trust. Except where the arrangements are undertaken carelessly, the argument is not thought to have much force; it would be considerably weakened if not eliminated altogether by ensuring that there is a long delay between the transfers into the trust and the later transfers to the children. Indeed, when you set up the seven trusts, you may have no immediate intention of transferring them to any particular person. You would be setting the scene so that if, at any later date, you wanted to transfer shares to your family, it could be done at a low tax cost. In these circumstances it would be extremely difficult for the Inland Revenue to maintain any argument at all that the arrangements were preordained.

The Family Home

One of the most significant assets most people possess is their home, and often it will be owned jointly by the husband and wife. This is usually advantageous because it may provide all the equalisation of value between the spouses that may be required. On the death of the first spouse, the survivor will usually inherit the half-interest owned by the deceased, either automatically if they own the house as joint tenants, or by will if they hold it as tenants in common. However, this can have most undesirable consequences on the second death.

For example:

A husband and wife own a house jointly, which is worth £250,000, and no other assets of significance. On the first death there is no inheritance tax because the husband's interest in the house passes to his widow and is exempt. However, on the death of the widow a charge to inheritance tax will arise because she will own the whole of the house. The excess of the value over £147,000 will be chargeable to tax at 40 per cent – a tax liability of £41,200.

If, on the death of the husband, his interest in the house had passed to his children, there would be no tax on his death because the value would be within the nil rate band of £147,000. On the death of his widow, her half of the house would pass to the children; that too will be within her nil rate band and no tax will arise. The tax of £41,200 is thus saved.

However, it may be that parents do not have sufficient trust and confidence in their children to allow the widow adequate security in these circumstances. She would be entitled to occupy the house by virtue of her joint ownership and the children could not insist on any rent in respect of her occupation, but they might insist on selling the house against their mother's wishes. This can be overcome by the husband and wife, during their lifetimes, entering into a mutual covenant binding on each other and their successors in title that the house would not be sold without the consent of both joint owners.

A possible difficulty with this arrangement is that the children who own half the house will not necessarily occupy it as their main residence, although as joint owners they would be entitled to do so. They will, therefore, not qualify for the private resident exemption for capital gains tax on their half of the house when it is eventually sold. This might not be a problem because they will have acquired their half at its market value on their father's death and indexation relief may be enough to eliminate all or most of the subsequent increase in value.

However, if there is likely to be a problem with capital gains tax, it would be better for the husband to leave his half-interest in trust for the children for life, with remainder to their mother if they predecease her. The house would still be treated as belonging to the children for inheritance tax purposes, but because their mother is a beneficiary of the settlement, the trustees could allow her to remain in the property. As I explained in detail in Chapter 6, this would be sufficient to preserve the capital gains tax exemption, as the house would be occupied as the main residence of a person entitled to occupy it under the terms of the settlement.

Great care is needed in drafting the settlement and in the exercise of the trustees' powers, because otherwise an interest in possession could inadvertently arise in favour of the mother, thereby bringing the whole of the house back into the estate of the mother for inheritance tax purposes.

Multiple Discretionary Trusts

Other possibilities arise in connection with discretionary trusts and saving inheritance tax. It would obviously be very helpful to have a number of discretionary trusts, each with their own nil rate band. You could divide up your estate into parcels of £147,000, each held by discretionary trust and no tax would arise on their ultimate distribution. Unfortunately, this does not work because the second discretionary trust will not gain any benefit from the nil rate band of £147,000 which is used up on the first transfer. The second transfer will be fully chargeable at the lifetime rates of tax. Nor does it help to make all the settlements on the same day (during lifetime or on death), because the nil rate band will effectively be divided between them.

However, what you can do is to put into discretionary trust assets of very low value (within your annual exemptions) which will grow in value later. In that way there will be no previous chargeable or potentially exempt transfers which could later be taken into account and each discretionary trust will have its own nil rate band. This can save a large amount of tax by multiplying the value of the nil rate band, but you do have to plan a long time in advance – and the growth in value of the settled property has to be significant. But if you plan early enough it will be.

Another means of achieving the same objective is by a combination of lifetime planning and a deed of variation. There will be cases where a person dies without a surviving spouse or any other available exemption and all his estate will be chargeable. The creation of a number of discretionary trusts on his death will save no tax on his estate, nor for his successors, because all settlements made on the same day (whether they are made by a will or by deed of variation) are treated as related settlements and, effectively, the tax will be the same on distributions out of each trust as if he had created a single trust.

If, however, during his lifetime he set up a series of discretionary trusts, say five discretionary trusts all with £1,000 on different days, a transfer on his death of £146,000 to each of the settlements would be extremely advantageous for his successors. The tax on his death would remain the same, but each of the discretionary trusts would have £146,000 of assets; and because none of them would have been created on the same day they would not be related settlements. They would therefore each be entitled to their nil rate band. A distribution out of each settlement would therefore give rise to no tax, so that the successors effectively have a £735,000 tax-free money box. There is no reason why this cannot be done by deed of variation so that the exact amount to obtain the maximum advantage can be precisely calculated.

Businesses

Business Property Relief

Business property relief is a special relief which applies when computing values for inheritance tax. It applies to business property of various descriptions and reduces the burden of tax on family businesses, so that they are not destroyed by over-whelming tax charges when they pass to the next generation.

Before the Budget on 10 March, if you had a business, or if you had more than 25 per cent of the shares in your family trading company, the relief was 50 per cent; if your shareholding (including that of your wife) was 25 per cent or less you were entitled to only 30 per cent relief. You also receive 30 per cent business relief on any property you owned which was used for the purposes of the business, or for the business of a company which you (and your wife) controlled.

The March 1992 Budget proposed a substantial extension to the scope of this relief. If the changes are enacted the 50 per cent relief will be increased to 100 per cent, hereby effectively providing complete exemption from inheritance tax on these types of property. The 30 per cent relief will go up to 50 per cent and there are some other changes as well, but they do not really affect the ideas discussed below. Whatever the rates of relief you should make the most of it. In many cases the relief will apply automatically, but there will be certain circumstances in which it will not and you should make a few rearrangements to your affairs to make sure that you get the maximum relief, rather than none at all.

For example, if you own the business premises from which the company trades, but you have given away some of the company's shares to take you below the control threshold (so that your shares can be valued on a minority basis), you will have shot yourself in the foot. You may have obtained a reduced valuation for your shares because you no longer control the company, but you will have deprived yourself of business property relief at 30 per cent on the value of the business premises. You need more than 50 per cent of the shares to qualify for relief on the property.

However, all is not lost. Although there is a minimum 2-year period before assets qualify for business relief, this does not apply to the shares which qualify you for business relief on the property. Accordingly, if you want to give property away you must get hold of sufficient shares to take you *beyond* the control threshold. As previously explained, these could be acquired by your wife so that they represent related property and they can be given away later without difficulty. When you give the property away it will qualify for business relief at 50 per cent and substantially reduce the value of the transfer for inheritance tax purposes.

However, your situation may be slightly different. You may own the property and you may also own most of the shares in the company that uses the property. This will enable you to claim 50 per cent business relief on the property, which you may feel is entirely satisfactory.

However, the position could be greatly improved if you were simply to give the property to the company. This may sound dramatic, but if you own most of the shares it will make very little difference. Provided that the property is used for the company's trade, no capital gains tax would apply on the transfer to the company, nor would any stamp duty arise. There would be a transfer of value for inheritance tax purposes, but this would depend on how many shares were held by others. The effect would be that you no longer own the property; the company would own the property and the value of the company's shares would therefore go up. The complex means by which shares in private companies are valued means that the value of the shares would not go up as much as the value of the property, and this would therefore cause value to disappear entirely. However, even if the shares increased in value exactly corresponding to the value of the property, the whole of the value of the shares, including this, increases the benefit from 100 per cent business relief and not just the 50 per cent which applied to the property. With a valuable business property the saving here can obviously be quite spectacular.

One More Share

You may have given away your shares to your family leaving yourself with only 25 per cent; this will be good from a share valuation point of view because a 25 per cent holding is worth comparatively little. For most company law purposes a 51 per cent holding is required for effective control of the company, but in some special cases you need 75 per cent of the votes. A person with only 25 per cent of the shares cannot therefore prevent the passing of a special resolution (which requires 75 per cent of the votes) and this has a substantial devaluing effect on the value of the shares. The trouble is that with only 25 per cent of the shares you only qualify for business relief at 50 per cent. You need one more share so that your shares qualify for the full 100 per cent relief. You do not need to have this share for very long, but you do need it.

Accordingly, if you are thinking about giving some of your remaining shares away, you need to get hold of one more share before you do so. Then whatever you give away will benefit from the 100 per cent relief.

Under the circumstances, and bearing in mind your intentions, it may be very likely that somebody would be only too happy to give one more share to enable you to obtain the higher relief. It is, however, important that the gift of the one share is entirely genuine and does not carry any obligation that the share will be given back later. If possible it would be much better if your wife were to obtain this single share; in that way it will be counted towards your shareholding for the purpose of calculating the business relief, but no problem would arise with reciprocity.

Deferred Shares

If you have a valuable family company you may be concerned about how to pass it on to the next generation. You may want to continue to run the company and enjoy all the profits, but your plan in due course is to pass it on to your family. Various possibilities have been mentioned above whereby shares can be transferred into trusts, but there is another technique which can be used; the issue of deferred shares.

You could issue a new class of deferred shares which would have no immediate value, but which would gradually grow in value in future years. The deferred shares would have no present voting rights, nor any rights to dividend, nor would they be entitled to any surplus in a winding up. Shares without these rights are clearly of no value, so that you may wonder what earthly use there is in issuing them at all. However, if the shares were to become entitled to full rights, ranking equally with the ordinary shares after the expiry of, say, 15 years, you can see that in 15 years they will become extremely valuable.

Depending on how many shares are issued they could completely swamp the existing shares. However, 15 years is a long time and they would have very little value at the moment. The company might go bust in the meantime or anything might happen to prevent this value crystallising at the end of the period. However, as each year passes, the deferred shares will gradually become more valuable, because the time will be drawing closer when they will rank equally with the ordinary shares.

If, therefore, you give these shares away to your children now, the value of the gift will be negligible and no inheritance tax would arise. When the value rises in 15 years' time there will be no occasion of charge and the transfer of value would be complete.

This is important for inheritance tax purposes, because it is the value of the gift when the shares are *given away* which is the measure of the gift, not the growth in value over the subsequent years. In this way the whole of the value can be passed to your children over a period without doing anything else. After 15 years the shares will be valuable and your shares will be worthless, and the value will have been removed from your estate without a charge to tax.

However, you do have to be very careful with this. You must avoid any possibility of a reservation of benefit and you must also ensure that the rights attaching to these shares do not enable you to prevent the value passing into the deferred shares in due course. Obviously, if in the 14th year you were still able to pay a huge dividend or to wind up the company and take all the assets yourself, the rights attaching to your existing shares, even at this late stage, would still be extremely valuable. Your failure to take such action, thereby allowing value to pass out of them, will be regarded as a gift which will be chargeable to tax.

The Inland Revenue has recently announced that it does not accept that a deferred share scheme along these lines is effective. They say that when the deferred shares gain all their rights after the 15-year period, they will regard that as an occasion of charge. Their view is widely regarded as unsound where the above precautions are taken, but the fact that they are seeking to challenge the position must act as a warning. It is therefore imperative that good professional advice be obtained to ensure that the procedures are undertaken with full regard to the Inland Revenue's view.

Employee Trusts – The Holy Grail?

One of the problems with inheritance planning is its interaction with capital gains tax. I have already explained that on death all a person's assets are revalued for capital gains tax, but no charge to capital gains tax arises; inheritance tax is chargeable on the estate anyway and perhaps two charges to tax on the same assets is thought to be rather unfair. This capital gains tax-free uplift is extremely valuable and should never be overlooked, even where holdover relief is available; you could end up much worse off than you think.

If you make a gift during your lifetime (whether you hold over the capital gain or not), you will not own the asset at your death and it will not be revalued for capital gains tax purposes. If you die within 3 years of making the gift you will have saved no inheritance tax at all, and you will have lost the tax-free uplift. This is called negative tax planning – or how to create tax liabilities out of thin air.

What you want is to have the best of both worlds – that is to have the assets revalued tax free for capital gains tax, but without any inheritance tax becoming payable either. This is the tax planners' equivalent of finding the Holy Grail.

We will assume that you own all the shares in your valuable family company. Neither your wife nor your children has any shares in the company and you would like them to inherit your shares, but without the inevitable tax liability. You may have left it all a bit late because you cannot be confident of surviving for 7 more years. You therefore run the risk of making a gift, saving no inheritance tax but losing the capital gains tax-free uplift. You can leave the shares to your spouse but the inheritance tax will simply be deferred until her death. What you want is an exemption. There isn't one, so you have to go looking for one which has a loophole through which you can squeeze.

The answer to this problem may well be an employee trust.

There is an exemption from inheritance tax for transfers of a controlling shareholding in a company to a discretionary trust for the exclusive benefit of the company's employees and directors. Unfortunately, some employees are disqualified from benefiting under the trust – those who are shareholders (unless they have less than 5 per cent) and those who are connected with a shareholder and anybody who had been a shareholder within the last 10 years. This effectively rules out the whole family, because connected persons for this purpose include spouses, lineal ancestors, and descendants and their spouses.

However, a deceased person is not connected with anybody, so if an employee trust is established by will and none of the rest of the family holds any shares, there is nothing to prevent them from being able to benefit under such an employee trust.

It is, of course, necessary for all (or nearly all) the employees to be beneficiaries of the trust, but there is no rule requiring any particular employee to receive any benefit from the trust. However, if by doing this you can avoid inheritance tax on the whole of the value of the company it would be a little mean not to allow your employees who are not members of your family some benefit. Indeed, it would also be tactically sensible to do so to avoid provoking the Inland Revenue unnecessarily.

An effective employee trust can enable the controlling shareholder to keep his shares in the company (and all the rights that go with them), safe in the knowledge that by his will, the transfer of the shares to this trust will create an exemption, thereby avoiding inheritance tax completely.

While the shares are retained by the trust there will be none of the periodic charges which normally apply to discretionary trusts, nor when the settled property is distributed will there be the normal exit charge. However, if events should occur which deprive the trust of its privileged status, an exit charge would arise, but it would be negligible – approximately 1 per cent for each year that the trust has been in existence.

It can get better. Because the deceased would have retained the shares until his death they will be revalued at market value on his death and if the family wished to sell the company after the death of the controlling shareholder, no capital gains tax would arise – unless, of course, the shares had increased in value *since* the date of death. Accordingly, a sale and a distribution of the sale proceeds to the family would give rise to neither inheritance tax nor capital gains tax and the tax-free transfer of the whole of the cash value of the company to the children would be complete.

Deed of Variation

If the shares in the company would qualify for the 100 per cent business property relief the creation of an employee trust in this way would not achieve a great deal because the shares in the company would effectively be exempt from inheritance tax anyway. However there will be many cases where the 100 per cent relief will not apply (and indeed it may never be introduced) and an employee trust may be a good solution. Furthermore, what about the position of a person who died before 10 March 1992 – the extended business property relief would not be available to him. You may also think that it would be a bit late for him to avoid the tax by transferring his shares to an employee trust – but that is to ignore the possibility of a deed of variation.

Deeds of variation are explained at length in the following pages but essentially the idea is that the beneficiaries of the deceased's estate can vary the will to create a better tax position. If they do it correctly, the terms of the deed of variation are treated as if they were the terms of the will itself. Accordingly it would be possible to rewrite the will so that on the death the shares in the company pass to an employee trust in exactly the manner as set out above and it would be just as effective as if the deceased had made the transfer himself.

Double Charges Regulations

The complexities of inheritance tax mean that it is quite possible for the tax to be artificially increased as well as reduced. For example, if you transfer £100,000 to a discretionary trust in which you are a beneficiary, you will make a chargeable transfer of £100,000, but you will not have diminished your estate at all, because you have reserved a benefit. The chargeable transfer to the discretionary trust will still be counted as a gift and, if you die within 3 years, you will have actually increased your estate by £100,000. Fortunately there are some special regulations known as the double charges regulations which protect you from effectively being charged to tax twice on the same amount. This relief (like most reliefs) also gives rise to some scope for tax saving.

For example:

Let us assume that a father makes a potentially exempt transfer to his son of a house worth £150,000, and because of his age or illness the father does not think that he will survive for 3 years. If the son were then to sell the house back to the father for, say, £100,000 it would look as if the father has increased his estate. He will have the property back in his estate, but the potentially exempt transfer he made earlier will still be counted if he dies within 3 years.

However, the double charges regulations come to the rescue and eliminate the property from his estate – although, of course, the £150,000 potentially exempt transfer will remain as part of his cumulative total of lifetime transfers. This would effectively put the father back in the same position – except that he had paid £100,000 for the property to his son and this £100,000 has gone from his estate. By this technique the father's estate is reduced by £100,000 and no 7-year survival period is necessary.

Gifts to Charity

The recently introduced provisions for gift aid, which allow tax relief for certain cash donations to charities, contains a loophole which can be exploited to gain a multiple tax deduction. The idea of gift aid is that the donation to the charity is treated as a net payment after deduction of basic rate tax, but if you pay tax at the higher rate you obtain full relief at higher rate as well.

For example:

If you give £750 to a charity, it will be treated as a gross gift of £1,000 from which you have had tax relief by deduction of £250. The charity can reclaim this tax from the Inland Revenue. You are entitled to a further £150 of tax relief to bring your total relief up to 40 per cent.

Gift aid does not apply to gifts made on death, but for inheritance tax gifts to charities are exempt anyway, so such a gift benefits from inheritance tax relief, also at 40 per cent.

However, it is possible to contrive both income tax and inheritance tax relief in respect of the same gift.

For example:
If you leave (say) £750 to somebody in your will, having made it known that this £750 is to be transferred to a charity, if the donee makes the payment to the charity within 2 years of your death, it will be treated as a gift by you and will be exempt from inheritance tax on your death. But there is nothing to stop the donee also claiming that he has made a gift aid donation and seeking income tax relief for the payment.

The charity will receive £750 from the donee, deemed to be under deduction of tax of £250 which it can reclaim from the Inland Revenue. The donee will be able to reclaim tax of £150 and the deceased's estate will save tax of 40 per cent of £750 which is £300.

The total of the charity's tax repayment of £250, the donee's extra tax relief of £150 and the inheritance tax saving of £300, amounts to a total tax saving of £700 on a gift of £750!

Wills and Deeds of Variation

Various studies have shown that comparatively few people bother to make a will. It is not that they do not want one, but just that they have not yet got round to dealing with it. They may hope fondly that everything will probably go to their spouse anyway, so it is not an urgent matter. This is a very misguided approach, because the legal rules which apply on intestacy can have a most unfortunate effect and your estate can pass to people whom you had no intention of benefiting. Furthermore, it can give rise to a charge to inheritance tax which you did not want either.

It is inappropriate here to go into these rules, except to point to some tax advantages which can be achieved by drawing up a will and what your heirs can do to obtain tax advantages even if you have not done so.

When somebody dies the executors read the will and in due course they pay out all the estate to those named as beneficiaries. It may be, however, that the beneficiaries realise that a tax advantage has been lost and it could have been much better if the will had said something else. Before they start gnashing their teeth about what the deceased should have done, they should consider the possibility of making a deed of variation. A deed of variation is a written document signed by the beneficiaries which effectively rewrites the will. Provided it is done within 2 years of the death (and the necessary notifications are made to the Inland Revenue), it is fully effective for inheritance tax and capital gains tax.

You could have a situation where the husband dies leaving everything by his will to his wife. I have already explained how this would waste the nil rate band, because he could have left £147,000 to his children (or to a discretionary trust for the family) without any tax being payable and that would save tax on £147,000 on the wife's death. So you enter into a deed of variation rewriting the will so that it does exactly that.

However, the situation could be entirely the reverse – the husband dies leaving everything to the children and nothing to the wife (who may have plenty of money of her own). If his estate is more than £147,000, some real tax will be payable. The children could enter into a deed of variation so that everything over £147,000 passes to the wife instead (and is exempt), thereby saving all the tax. The wife would then be in a position, if she chose to do so, to make lifetime gifts to her children of a similar amount; the gifts would be potentially exempt transfers and if she were to survive for 7 years they would be wholly exempt. The overall objective of the deceased's will would have been achieved, but in a slightly different fashion, without any tax arising. It is essential that a deed of variation is not conditional on the making of the lifetime gifts or undertaken for any kind of consideration, but this is usually unlikely to be a problem.

For the same reason another loophole arises from the use of a deed of variation. Let us assume that a husband dies, leaving the whole of his £250,000 estate to his wife, but within 2 years the value of the estate has grown to £350,000. The widow could enter into a deed of variation by which she takes a specific legacy of £250,000, the residue passing to the children. The whole of the chargeable estate will therefore be exempt, because the full amount of £250,000 will pass to the spouse, leaving the £100,000 passing to the children entirely free of inheritance tax. This is effectively a means of excluding the increase in value from the widow's estate without causing her to make a transfer at all.

It is not necessary to get anybody's agreement before a deed of variation can be made. Anybody who benefits from somebody's estate on death can make a deed of variation to redirect his inheritance elsewhere. Nobody's consent is needed, nor indeed do you need to tell anybody, except the Inland Revenue. It is usually helpful to tell the executors, because it will assist them in administering the estate, but you do not need their consent. Obviously it is better if everybody agrees, because then it can be much more effective and comprehensive, but if they do not agree, you can always deal with your inheritance on your own.

Anybody drawing up a will should bear in mind the possibility that the tax rules may change and a deed of variation may become desirable after their death. They should therefore carefully consider whether to include legacies to infants because an infant cannot make a deed of variation – he does not have the legal capacity to do so. An application can be made to the courts to order a variation on behalf of an infant and the courts will usually do so, providing it is for the infant's benefit. However, it is an expensive process and something to be avoided if possible.

It should also be understood that even if you have not made a will it is still possible for those who would benefit under the intestacy rules to vary the devolution of the estate in exactly the same way.

What About Income Tax?

However, you cannot do everything with a deed of variation. Although they are very effective for inheritance tax and capital gains tax, they are not at all helpful for income tax.

You will remember the general rule that the income of a child is taxed on the parent, if the parent provided the capital giving rise to the income. You may think that it would be a good idea to vary the rule to transfer lump sums to your own children. They could enjoy the income (or you could spend it on them for their benefit) and obtain the benefit of their personal allowances to avoid the income tax arising.

Unfortunately this will not work, because the rule whereby the transfer by deed of variation is deemed to have been made by the deceased does not apply for income tax, and because you will be treated as having provided the funds for your children and any income arising to them will be taxed on you. This is one reason why having a will is helpful. If the rule provides that the money passes directly to the grandchildren, the rules for the aggregation of children's income with that of their parents will not apply and the children's personal allowances will be able to be set against their income. This can be extremely useful. Personal allowances are now £3,445, so if you have three children this will enable you to have over £10,000 per annum tax free to be used for the maintenance, education and benefit of the children.

Wills and Discretionary Trusts

The best of all worlds is to draft a will to provide that everything goes into a discretionary trust on your death so that your executors can distribute the assets as they see fit, having regard to the tax rules at the time. There is a special relief which provides that distributions out of such a trust within 2 years of death will be treated as having been made by the deceased; it is a sort of built-in deed of variation, but without any of the disadvantages. It is necessary to have the utmost faith in your executors as they are going to make these decisions, but if for example the surviving spouse (who may have inherited most of the estate anyway) is one executor and your professional adviser is the other, everything should be entirely satisfactory. The testator can, of course, provide how the estate should be distributed if nothing is done within the 2-year period or if the executors do not agree. With this safeguard, and by providing a letter of wishes (an informal, non-binding indication of his preferences), the testator may feel happy that his estate will be distributed in exactly the manner he would have liked, and with the best tax advantages.

Obtaining Further Exemptions

Deeds of variation are also effective for capital gains tax and this can give rise to further advantages. A situation sometimes arises where a person dies owning a property and during the administration of the estate the property is sold at a profit. This can easily happen for two reasons. The first is that the executors are normally keen to agree a comparatively low value for the property for inheritance tax purposes, because that will naturally reduce the tax liability. The second reason is that it can sometimes take some time for the estate to be administered and for the assets to be sold; in the mean time the value might have gone up. The result is that the executors end up with a capital gains tax liability, unless of course the property passed to somebody who was using it as their main residence. The executors will have an annual exemption of £5,800 to set against the gain, but that may not do them a lot of good. What is needed is a way of obtaining further exemptions.

A deed of variation can be extremely helpful in these circumstances. Let us assume that the residue of the estate is left to the deceased's three children. They could execute a deed of variation in respect of this property so that it does not fall into residue, but passes as a specific legacy to themselves in equal shares absolutely. When the property is sold it is they who make the capital gain and three annual exemptions will be available to set against the gain. They might decide to go further and include their own children so that the property passes to them and the grandchildren in equal shares absolutely. The grandchildren's annual exemptions would also be available to set against the gain. The grandchildren's share of the property would belong to them absolutely and could not be taken by their parents for their own benefit. However, if the grandchildren are infants, the funds could quite properly be used for their maintenance, education and benefit during their lifetime.

A tax case (known as *Marshall* v. *Kerr* – still running at the time of writing) recently decided that, although for capital gains tax purposes the deceased is treated as making the dispositions under the deed of variation, that is not enough to prevent the person making the deed of variation a settlor of the settlement as well. If this case continues to be decided in the Inland Revenue's favour it will not be possible to set up an effective non-resident trust by deed of variation. The person making the deed would be a settlor and all the gains of the non-resident trustees would be deemed to accrue to him and be taxed accordingly.

If, however, the non-resident trust was established by will, there would be no danger of anybody else being treated as a settlor and although it may benefit all the members of the family, the new rules would not apply; the gains of the non-resident trustees would not be chargeable to capital gains tax in the hands of the trustees, but only the beneficiaries to the extent that they received capital payments from the trust in accordance with the pre-March 1991 rules.

AFTERWORD

I hope that the ideas contained in this book will enable all readers to achieve a legitimate reduction in their tax liabilities. Some of the techniques are appropriate to those with substantial wealth, but a number of the suggestions are equally applicable to those with more modest means. It is inevitable that some of the ideas will be criticised by professional advisers, who would prefer to take the initiative and *not* have their clients coming to them with tax saving ideas! They may feel an implied criticism that they should have got there first. No such criticism is appropriate. Even the most eminent tax advisers are always alert and responsive to ideas from others, and the 'not invented here' response does no service to the client. You should not be discouraged or put off by such an approach.

Just because an alternative view can be put forward does not mean that a particular tax saving proposal will not work. Each needs to be examined critically in the light of individual circumstances, and sometimes it will be necessary to argue the points vigorously with the Inland Revenue. I should add that this book is essentially a distillation of many years of experience advising on these matters, and readers should approach any tax saving proposals based on these ideas with vigour and confidence.

INDEX

Piatkus Business Books

Piatkus Business Books have been created for people like you, busy executives and managers who need expert knowledge readily available in a clear and easy-to-follow format. All the books are written by specialists in their field. They will help you improve your skills quickly and effortlessly in the workplace and on a personal level.

Each book is packed with ideas and good advice which can be put into practice immediately. Titles include:

General Management Skills

Be Your Own PR Expert Bill Penn
Brain Power: The 12-Week Mental Training Programme
  Marilyn vos Savant and Leonore Fleischer
The Complete Time Management System Christian H. Godefroy
  and John Clark
Confident Decision Making J. Edward Russo and
  Paul J. H. Schoemaker
Dealing with Difficult People Roberta Cava
The Energy Factor: How to Motivate Your Workforce Art McNeil
**Firing On All Cylinders: Tried and Tested Techniques to Improve
  the Performance of Your Organisation** Jim Clemmer with
  Barry Sheehy
How to Develop and Profit from Your Creative Powers
  Michael LeBoeuf
**The Influential Manager: How to Use Company Politics
  Constructively** Lee Bryce
Leadership Skills for Every Manager Jim Clemmer and
  Art McNeil
Managing Your Team John Spencer and Adrian Pruss
Problem Solving Techniques that Really Work Malcolm Bird
Your Memory: How It Works and How to Improve It
  Kenneth L. Higbee

Sales and Customer Services

The Art of the Hard Sell Robert L. Shook
How to Close Every Sale Joe Girard
How to Succeed in Network Marketing Leonard S. Hawkins
How to Win Customers and Keep Them for Life Michael LeBoeuf
Selling by Direct Mail John W. Graham and Susan K. Jones
The Selling Edge: Tactics for Winning a Sale Every Time
  Patrick Forsyth
Telephone Selling Techniques that Really Work Bill Good